Praise for 'Finding Paradise After the Storm'

"'Finding Paradise After the Storm' is a beautifully written book interwoven with inspirational messages in the face of some tatarus life experiences. Ms. Caza's tale of survival is harrowing, engrossing, and commands the reader's attention every step of the way. It is a testamental body of evidence that shows how one can overcome verbal & physical abuse. Caza's book is also a first class ticket for those seeking to advance their spiritual evolution." – Ryan McCormick, Executive Producer of the *Outer Limits of Inner Truth Radio Show*

"Lisa Caza has written a thoughtful, energetic book which combines her triumph as a domestic warrior and her gifts as a channeler and healer. I recommend 'Finding Paradise After the Storm' to everyone interested in healing and how the spirit lifts us up." – Constance Stellas, Author of *The Astrology Gift Guide* and *Advanced Astrology for Life*

"Lisa Caza shows the world how to be strong, resilient, smart and stunning through the worst of crises. She holds her head high and pushes on like a Queen. She shows the reader how to live this life (even under the most dangerous of circumstances) beautifully and insight-fully. This woman is tough, no victim here!" – Laura Lyn, Author of *Healing With the Angel Rays* and *The ABC'S of Psychic Development*

"Every once in a while you come across a book that speaks to your heart and soul. Lisa Caza's 'Finding Paradise After the Storm' has done just that! She has an amazing ability to bring you right into her personal traumas and then guides you to her triumphs. It's a wonderful page turner. Caza shows you how to become the 'Phoenix Rising' within your own life. Her book gives you the tools that humanity needs NOW! Whether you experienced abuse or you are on a path of creating your own paradise, this book is a Must Have!" – Kerrie O'Connor, Psychic Medium and Creator of the *Trinity Love Activation Works*.

"While I consider Lisa a distant sister to me, the intimacies she shares with the world in this book are both beautiful and bold. *Finding Paradise After the Storm* is a recounting of memories that I know have been painful to share, however, as one of the people who urged Lisa to write a book, I am happy that she moved forward with this important mission. It is my genuine hope that other women who may be struggling or searching for answers can find solace in these pages. Lisa has lived through some extreme trials, but in the end, she has surfaced stronger and more skilled in her craft, willing and able to help those who seek her help." – Tamara Dorris, Author of *The Law of Distraction and Art of Intention*.

Finding Paradise
— After —
the Storm

Lisa Caza

BALBOA.
PRESS
A DIVISION OF HAY HOUSE

Balboa Press books may be ordered through booksellers or by contacting:

Balboa Press
A Division of Hay House
1663 Liberty Drive
Bloomington, IN 47403
www.balboapress.com
1 (877) 407-4847

Because of the dynamic nature of the Internet, any web addresses or
links contained in this book may have changed since publication and
may no longer be valid. The views expressed in this work are solely those
of the author and do not necessarily reflect the views of the publisher,
and the publisher hereby disclaims any responsibility for them.

The author of this book does not dispense medical advice or prescribe
the use of any technique as a form of treatment for physical, emotional,
or medical problems without the advice of a physician, either directly
or indirectly. The intent of the author is only to offer information
of a general nature to help you in your quest for emotional and
spiritual well-being. In the event you use any of the information in
this book for yourself, which is your constitutional right, the author
and the publisher assume no responsibility for your actions.

Any people depicted in stock imagery provided by Thinkstock are
models, and such images are being used for illustrative purposes only.
Certain stock imagery © Thinkstock.

Print information available on the last page.

ISBN: 978-1-5043-4326-8 (sc)
ISBN: 978-1-5043-4327-5 (e)

Balboa Press rev. date: 03/14/2018

Dedications

To my found paradise: my wonderful husband
and soulmate life partner ... who always
unconditionally loves, encourages, and supports
me. Without him and the light that he shines in
my life, essentially this book may not have existed.

To my spirit guides; for giving me the
guidance and insight that I've needed
throughout the years, and for the astoundingly
unconditional love and support that they
always show me ... even when I'm sure I've
caused them to do countless face palms.

Contents

About the Book ix

Preface xi

The Experience 1

The Night of Reckoning 73

The Journey Part One: In Limbo 89

The Journey Part Two: Survival of the
    Fittest & Pursuing Dreams 108

The Journey Part Three:
    New Relationships and Marriage 130

Lessons Learned & Guidance to Follow:
    Finding Paradise 144

- Create Change Before Divine Steps In 145
- Have Patience With Yourself and
    Your Processes 147
- Ignore & Overcome Fears 150
- Don't Idly Wait for Miracles 152
- Ask for Help & Direction From Your
    Angels and Guides 154
- Listen To & Follow Your Intuition
    and Divine Guidance 157
- Nurture Yourself: Self Love &
    Pursuing Interests 158
- Change Your Search Methods &
    Criteria 161

- The Law of Attraction &
  Reprogramming the Mind 165
- Let Go & Forgive Yourself and Others 168
Life Path Divine Sequential Order:
  Everything Happens for a Reason 171
Paradise Found: New Love Relationships
  & How to Make Them Succeed 182
- Every Love Will Be Different 182
- There is No Comparison 183
- Let Go of the Controlling Reins 185
- Self-Awareness 188
- Open & Honest Communication 189
- The Tug-of-War 192
- Pick Your Battles 194
Other Points of Interest & Insight to
  Remember 196
- Like a Sponge Sopping Up the
  'Good Stuff' 196
- Life Path Divine Sequential Order –
  Take Two 199
- Developing Psychic Abilities Amidst
  the Chaos 200
- Don't Give Your Personal Power
  Over to Psychics 205
Meditation to Meet Your Spirit Guides 208
A Final Word About My Journey 212
About the Author 221

About the Book

*I*n this inspiring partial memoir, internationally-known clairvoyant psychic and media personality Lisa Caza shares her experience in detail as a surviving warrior of domestic violence and how she, with the help of her spirit guides and Divine, rebuilt herself and finally connected with her divinely intended life partner. Lisa then reveals profound divine insight, guidance and lessons that she learned throughout her journey in order to help guide others towards finding their own successful love relationships. She especially wishes for everyone to realize that there is a relationship paradise waiting for them – if they want it. And the first steps towards that paradise is to choose happiness and pursue it.

While this book illustrates many important spiritual lessons and concepts (some of which are deeply embedded in the story itself and not always highlighted or openly obvious), it can teach everyone how to find their own divinely intended love partners ... their own little pieces of paradise. Whether you are a surviving warrior of domestic violence yourself, still trying to heal from a significant past relationship, or a spirit who has been long-yearning to find that very special someone, the insights and tips Lisa reveals will prove to be invaluable tools along your own journey towards paradise.

This book utilizes spiritual and psychic concepts to assist individuals in finding paradise after their storm.

Preface

"You will write a book," said Psychic Clara (or some other sort of name that started with the letter 'c'. I can't remember now as it was so long ago). That was in 1994.

"Lisa, you seriously need to write a book about your experiences," said a close friend merely four years later.

"You've got a book in you. You need to get it out and available to the public," said my late grandmother only a few months prior to her passing in 2000.

"Write a book! I know you have it in you," said a previous friend and fellow psychic advisor. That was in 2007.

Fast forward eight years. I thought that I had heard the last of those statements ... until one evening my phone rings. It's my publicist and manager:

"Hey Lisa. How are you? Oh crap! Hold on a minute I have a beep on the other line." I giggle to myself as I sit on hold and listen to the silence on the other end. Typical Ryan! He always has ten things on the go all at once. I seriously don't know how he can handle such chaos all the time. Apparently he thrives on it. Oh ... 'click' ... there he is ...

"Lisa, I have Laura Lynn on the line. She said that she had a vision about you. So let me talk to her to find out what it is and I'll call you right back. Hopefully it's something good!"

"Really? Okay then. And blah! It better be something good. Some good news is definitely welcomed right now."

Well, after ten minutes of waiting (which felt like an agonizing hour), Ryan called me back only to say the same darn thing! Laura said I need to write a book – and as soon as I can because we're going on tour soon. What? Again with the book writing!

Okay. Okay. I get it. I have to write a book! But the thing is over the years I've tried and tried to think about what to write. It's not like I've been purposely ignoring the divine messages all this time. I just didn't know HOW to write a book. And on what exactly? The most that I've been able to write the past few years has been the odd blog post here and there. You see, I would often get stuck because of the simple fact that my life hasn't been all that easy – a lot of my experiences could be rather unbelievable to some ... and it most certainly would take more than just one book. My usual reply to those folks telling me to write has been this: "A book? Holy Hannah my life wouldn't fit in just one book. It would fill up an entire SERIES of novels! Maybe a movie would be better? It would make an awesome horror/thriller flick."

But admittedly, every single person who relayed on that divine message to me was right. I mean, every day I work with people – helping to guide them along on their own life paths the best I can with my psychic gifts ... and usually also sharing some of my own life experiences to help inspire and motivate them. So why am I not getting this same information out there to others who may need a wee bit of help but don't know where to find me?

That has brought me up to the here and now ... and the writing of this book. It took me a while to gather up my courage ... and as I write this Preface there are still some cobwebs in this brain of mine that need clearing out. I'm sure I'll be all right as I go through this book.

It also took me a bit of time to figure out what this book was going to be about. As mentioned there are so many things that I could write or talk about. But how much of that would truly fit into a whole book? Perhaps in time I'll receive further divine guidance regarding that particular dilemma. But for now I have in fact been guided to talk about my experiences as a survivor of domestic violence, and how I rebuilt myself and my life afterwards ... especially as it pertains to the relationship area of life. Finding and getting involved in new relationships after experiencing an abusive partner – or even just after having gone through a rather difficult divorce or break-up – the idea of having another partner can be frightening ... and that's despite the strong, desperate yearning within our hearts, bodies and souls for one.

While this guidebook is geared towards all of the men and women warriors out there who are trying to rebuild themselves and their lives after leaving an abusive relationship or marriage, the majority of the insight and advice given will most definitely help all men and women alike who have hurt hearts from past relationship experiences.

For the first time ever, I will discuss some of my specific experiences while I was in my first marriage (which lasted a long fourteen years), as well as what I call "The Night of Reckoning": which was the very night that Divine showed me that It had enough and was stepping into the situation in order to make me get out of that place! From there I shall outline the first few days, months, and years of being a single parent; what I went through and what I had done. I will try to lead you to the present day as smoothly as I can. After my story has been told, I will then reveal specific spiritual "lessons," realizations, steps of guidance, profound concepts and insight for you to remember and take with you to use as you travel on your own journey. Hence the reason for this book.

As a forewarning, some of the details written regarding my experience when I was still in my first marriage may be troubling to some folks. I do apologize in advance for any upset as that is not my intention. However, as many of my clients already know: I tell the truth no matter how painful. Today I tell the truth – not to gain pity and most certainly not to give people the opportunity to judge. If you feel the desire to express pity or judge in any way, then I kindly ask that you read no further and close this book. I am not a victim. I am a warrior. Sincerely, with all my heart and soul, the *only* intention behind my telling this story is that of hopefully helping to inform, inspire, motivate, guide, and heal others. Nothing more.

Other than the names mentioned in this Preface, as well as my own, all names have been changed in order to preserve those individual's sense of privacy, including my current husband. Although my ex-husband has passed, I shall still likewise change his name out of respect for the departed. No matter what he had done to me in the past, I never wish ill will upon his spirit. So for those reasons, he will be known henceforth as "Mark."

This was my personal journey. It is my truth of what I experienced and how I learned and grew emotionally and spiritually. Ultimately, it is how my spiritual knowledge and personal divine guidance not only grew in strength over the years, but also how it truly helped me to rise above my perceived adversities and succeed. It is the story of a wounded healer transforming into the healed healer. It is my hopes that sharing this story will show you how to follow your own guidance. Remember that no matter how scary or difficult it may be at times, keep happiness as your main goal, ignore the fear, and plow forward so that you too can ultimately find your own piece of paradise after the storm.

The Experience

"*I* got a job offer in Vancouver. Are you going to come with me, or are you going to stay here? Either way I don't care what you do. But you need to make a decision fast because I'm leaving in two weeks."

That question right there was my very first fork in the road along my path. It was a major one. It was essentially a life-changing one. Yet here I was … only seventeen years old.

At the time I was so torn within: on one hand I was foolishly in love with this man and always wanted to be with him. Yet on the other hand I would be moving clear across the country; leaving all that I had ever known behind … including my horses, my dear grandmother and young teenage brother (of whom I had just been reunited with after a three-year separation). However, admittedly I also wasn't in the best of places emotionally-speaking when this ultimatum was sprung upon me: just six months prior I had given birth to my first child. Pressured by my family and her father (which was indeed Mark – who outright denied her), I was forced against my will to give her up for adoption. So I was still grappling with the trauma and overwhelming grief. I truly wasn't in any shape to make such an important, life-changing decision. I was a psychological and emotional mess! Well, my answer to that question ultimately formed the rest of my life. Despite my strong yearning to remain with my grandmother, I blindly accompanied him to Vancouver.

I still don't fully understand what truly caused me to choose that particular path. Was it the sex? Was it the financial security? Was it the free-spirited lifestyle of the hard-core biker with all the leather, Harley's, and parties? Was I searching for the loving father-figure that I never had (as I never knew my biological father and suffered horrible physical and sexual abuse as a young child and teen)? Or maybe it was all of the above? I don't know. I'm still trying to work that one out. However, as I write this, the human side of me thinks, "Isn't hindsight the greatest? Take a good long and hard look at that man's final statement to you! He didn't care what you did? Let me repeat: HE DID NOT CARE! He said it himself in those exact words. How was that showing you love? Good God Almighty woman! You certainly couldn't take the hint could you? God you were dumb at seventeen!"

That realization hit me like a ton of bricks. Wow … how obvious it is today, but yet I totally ignored it all those years ago. How could I have ignored that? No, I guess I couldn't take a hint. I mean, since I started dating Mark two years prior I had been given "signs" of what I should expect from him in future years: his controlling nature, the odd angry outbursts and flying fists, him falsely accusing me of sleeping around, and even a night of being battered over the head with a cheeseburger clenched in his fist because I flat-out denied his accusations.

Yes, you read that last example correctly. I suffered a cheeseburger beating simply because I refused to confess to something that I truly did not ever do. Why would I admit to doing something that I didn't do? Well, I have to admit that sadly enough, eventually Mark did finally manage to beat out of me what he wanted to hear. After an hour or more of what looked and felt like a torturing session out of the Tudor era, I finally gave in and gave him what he wanted. I confessed to the false "charge" of "treason against His Majesty's person."

I know what you're going to say. Why in God's name did you do such a thing? I'll tell you why: because I figured once he got what he wanted, then he would stop beating on me. He just wasn't accepting the actual truth for an answer. So after "confessing," I received one final beating over the head. In my mind at the time, I felt that I was proven right. But in looking back a number of years later I realized the true nature of the situation: in actuality I didn't give him a chance to beat on me any further because at that moment I had the opportunity to escape: all I remember is bolting out the back door like a race horse out of the starting gate. In my terrified panic I stumble and fall, and then do what can only be described as the most flawless acrobatic somersault. I didn't even minutely falter. I rolled out of that somersault without skipping a beat and continued sprinting full force (years later even Mark said that he was impressed at how "gracefully pro" I looked coming out of that roll). Having lost my glasses in my tumble, and with remnants of cheeseburger all throughout my long thick hair, I made my way uptown to the local bar where I knew some of our biker friends were hanging out. Ear-bursting country music and drunken maniacal laughter greeted me as I blasted through the door of the bar. I found my friends immediately: having a great time in the middle of the dance floor. I hollered out their names over the music to get their attention. They took one look at me and they all came running. Never mind the fact that a sixteen-year-old was in the bar. They were more concerned about my appearance: no glasses, lobster-red eyes from crying, hair matted with hamburger, cheese, ketchup and mustard, shirt torn and dirt covering my jeans and hands.

To make the story short here, they made me stay with them that night and they confronted Mark the next day. Bless their hearts they also managed to somehow find my glasses for me.

I don't know what those friends said to him, but all was well afterwards ... except for the huge goose egg that I developed on my head. Of course I "conveniently forgot" about the entire thing ... and for the most part so did he. That is until every so often, for reasons unknown, he would bring it up just to remind me of how "horrible" a person I was for having been unfaithful to him. Yes indeed. As you will eventually see, my coerced false confession would come around every so often and bite me in the rear end.

Chapter Two

So I decided to move out west with Mark. With my fate now sealed, truck loaded to the hilt, and the Harley safely secured on the trailer behind us, we drove the gruelling four days across the country. It was hard for me not to cry on and off for the first few days – for I just didn't know when, if ever, I'd return. All I could think about was my beloved grandmother and the unconditional love that I was leaving behind me: How could I leave my Nana? I just want my Nana. Why am I doing this? Please God ... please ... help me ...

Then, without warning, my stern (and much wiser) Higher Self spoke: "Well ... too late for that now isn't it? You're already half-way there. There's no turning back now. So suck it up buttercup. You made your decision. You have no choice in this now. You must follow through!" That definitely snapped me back to reality. At that point I hardened myself and my attitude; I shoved away the gut-wrenching emotional tugs at my breaking heart and didn't look back (as often).

For the most part, our life in Vancouver for the first year or two was actually wonderful ... in a rather weird sort of way. Initially, neither one of us knew a single soul – we were literally on our own at that point, and we were living in a motel room for about two weeks – until we found a basement apartment to rent. Essentially, being in this seemingly "alien world" brought the two of us closer together. It was almost like our life before didn't even exist ... including his angry outbursts, controlling nature, and beatings. It was as if he was a completely different person.

We went and did everything with each other; we were inseparable other than for when he had to go to work. Almost every day we would venture out on the Harley to explore all that this wondrous new world had to offer: the nightclubs, the never-ending twisting highways through the towering northern mountains, the ocean view ... did I mention the nightclubs? While I never did acquire the taste or liking for alcohol or drugs, this was one thing that never did change with Mark. He NEEDED his beer and drugs. He couldn't function without them. Not a day went by that he didn't have a beer in his hand or joint in his mouth at some point. And not a weekend went by that he didn't drink himself into quite the drunken stupor. In looking back, that was definitely another "clue" that I should have caught onto: it was such a huge difference between us. But ... naïve me I carried onwards. However, in my own defense I would have to say that I was likely "conditioned" at this point because all my life I was surrounded by crazed alcoholics. It was nothing new to me, and as a result I felt that drinking alcohol was just a part of life. In fact, at my very young age I was more impressed by it than anything else. How cool it was to hang out with a bunch of drunken bikers all the time! So I wasn't too bothered by the constant drinking. Until much later on ...

Life was going so well for the two of us in Vancouver that I was filled with such great hope and happiness. Our relationship was the most loving and cohesive relationship ever seen. Never before had Mark shown me such huge amounts of love, adoration, and protectiveness ... even in front of others! We were also doing quite well financially, making new friends, and progressing materially where we finally moved out of the basement apartment and found a cozy one-bedroom house to rent. I began to feel that I had made the right decision. After having worked at my telemarketing job for the last year, I even managed to save enough money to book a flight home to visit my grandmother for a few weeks. Yes! This life was pretty darn awesome!

Yeah ... okay Lisa hold that thought will you please?

Chapter Three

I had a routine that I followed whenever I had to go into work. I would always leave extra-early so that I'd arrive at least an hour early for my shift. I loved to do that because it not only got me focused and in the frame of mind to deal with my work duties, but I also liked to sit with my coffee, smoke up a storm and talk with some of my fellow employees. I did that for EVERY shift. Until one day ...

This particular day started out like any other, and I carried out my usual work routine of showing up an hour early. I grabbed my coffee and sat down at the usual table with my co-workers. I pull out a cigarette, put it in my mouth, and grab my lighter to light it. Oh hell. Hold up a second here. Ohhhh yuck I feel like crap all of a sudden.

Within I'd say a mere five seconds this entire inner argument then took place:

"What the hell? Why am I salivating so much? Oh god ... am I going to hurl all over the place here? What did I eat?"

"Lisa, you had better force yourself through it. Ignore this feeling and just light that damn cigarette before people start to notice that something is wrong."

"But I can't. I feel ill just thinking about lighting it."

"DO IT! DO IT DAMMIT!! You look like a complete moron staring into space with an unlit cigarette in your mouth. LIGHT IT NOW!"

It took almost all my strength to not vomit everywhere and light that cigarette. But I did as my inner self commanded. Magically, and just as quickly as what it had come on, the ill feeling totally disappeared as I took the first few drags off of my now lit smoke. I went through my entire shift without thinking about it again. In fact, I forgot about the entire thing for many days. The feeling never did return. And after all, I was preparing to head back home to see my beautiful grandmother! At this point it's been over two years since I last saw her. Going home was the only thought in this pea-sized brain. It's all that mattered to me right then. I was also eager to tell my grandmother all about the wonderful progress and happy life that we now have together.

A week later I find myself excitedly boarding a plane. Again I had a one-track mind:

"I'm going home! I'm going home! Oh thank God I get to see my Nana! Crap I forgot to bring some sanitary pads. I know my time of the month is coming any day. Oh forget it, I'll just pick some up on the way to my Nana's apartment. No big deal. I'll worry about that when I can do something about it."

At the mention of her name, immediately my thoughts focused right back onto my grandmother and how ecstatic I was to be going home to see her. As the plane flew over the snow-covered mountains and then the open prairies, I constantly stared out my window to watch the world below pass me by. Finding myself choking back tears a few times, my focus then turned to wondering what those tears were truly for. Realize over those last two and a half years I had grown and changed significantly – both spiritually and emotionally. I was becoming a little bit more aware of my own processes. I began to question: Was it just my sheer happiness with the fact that I was going home to see my grandmother? Was it because everything has worked out for the best? Was it because of how Mark made fun of me just a few hours prior because he "caught me" performing a tarot reading for a co-worker? I had no clue. But then my still immature self returned to the forefront of my consciousness: Bah! Why did I care? All I knew was that I was happy with my life, and happy to go home for a visit.

Well I will say right now that I should have cared ... and very much so. Today I have the full belief that those tears were an omen of sorts for things to come. My own Higher Self knew that "something was up" and that perhaps I was once again leaving behind something that was very dear to me. A life that I didn't know I'd ever return to again. Something was definitely up ... nothing was ever going to be the same. I just didn't realize it. Until a week later ...

Chapter Four

Sitting at my grandmother's kitchen table, again the tears were starting to well up and my anxiety level was sky-rocketing. I felt like my chest was being crushed by a fully-loaded transport truck, and I swear the only sound that I could hear in that moment was my own heart pounding a mile a minute. All I could think about was what would I do? What would HE do? All I could do was pray that all will be well and that I was overreacting. I tried to persuade myself that maybe I was just late. It happened to me before. So perhaps that's all it is ...

With my grandmother, my two cousins, and an old high school friend of mine staring at me expectantly, I picked up the small paper bag that I held in my lap. I didn't see the result yet. I wanted to be surrounded by those who loved and supported me as I did so. I closed my eyes, reached into the bag, and pulled it out. I opened my eyes once more and nervously peered down:

The result was clear as day. There was no misreading it. Two lines. Positive. I saw it. I nodded my head. Then ... utter complete blackness enveloped me ...

Upon waking the first thing that entered my conscious brain was that I was pregnant. And ... I was in sheer panic and fright. I remembered how "well-received" my last pregnancy was with Mark and the family. I highly doubted that this second pregnancy would be any different. Except for one thing: I made a solemn vow to myself and my first-born child as I held her that I would *never* be forced to give up any other children for adoption *ever* again. And abortion was completely out of the question for I didn't believe in it at the time. It just wasn't an option for me personally. So there was only one option left: I was keeping this beautiful child. I was going to do whatever I could in my power to protect him or her. And that was THE bottom line.

I glanced around at everyone surrounding me. My grandmother was speaking, but I couldn't make out what she was saying. I was still so fogged from my fainting spell. Then my one cousin looked at me sternly, took me by my shoulders and gently shook me to snap me back into some semblance of reality. Once she saw that my eyes were more focused she went on to say,

"Lisa, whatever you want to do please know that we will do whatever we can to help you. Don't worry about what Mark says. You are number one right now."

I just silently nodded my head to acknowledge her support. At this point I couldn't make direct eye contact with anyone in the room. I was just way too fully absorbed with all of the "what if" questions that were swirling about in my mind. All the memories of what I went through with my first pregnancy, as well as of course Mark's past behaviors, attitudes and beatings that I had suffered came flooding back to me. I knew with every bone in my body that this was NOT going to go too well.

While I was completely engulfed in the whirlwind that was my thoughts, my grandmother, cousins and school chum took their respective turns talking to me. I hardly remember anything that they had said – except for one very bold statement that my friend himself made to me. It literally snapped me right out of that swirling, out-of-control whirlwind. If anyone knew the trials I had so far endured with Mark, well it would be him for he witnessed some of it. I will never forget his words:

"If that bastard does anything to you, you damn well call me! I don't care what time of the day or night it is. You pick up that phone! And if you need a place to stay, then you can stay with me and my girlfriend. Your Nana and I will make sure that you get home here. I promise you that. And we'll take care of you. But right now, you have only a few days before you have to go back and face him. So try to put it out of your mind the best you can and enjoy the remainder of your time here."

For the next few days I did the best I could to listen to my concerned friend and implement those words of wisdom. But it was hard. I often found myself thinking about having to inform Mark of my pregnancy, and feeling utter dread towards the "consequences."

As the hour came for me to return to Vancouver, I remember pausing for as long as I possibly could at the security gate in the airport. I looked back at my grandmother and cousin who were standing there, waiting to see me off. Of course I knew that I didn't have telepathic powers, but with all my might I was trying to send the messages to them to stop me from crossing the security check ... to stop me from boarding that plane. Obviously my "telepathic messages" weren't received; they weren't budging an inch. Yet I could hesitate no longer for I was starting to clearly irritate the passengers trying to walk past me. At that point I resigned myself to the inevitable, and with tears flowing blew kisses goodbye to the two of them, turned around and walked through the gate. Once more I leave my beloved security and unconditional love behind me.

Chapter Five

"*U*hm, I need to talk to you about something." I was so nervous I could barely breathe (which definitely isn't a good thing for a person who has asthma). A few days have passed since my return to Vancouver. I needed that time to muster up the strength and courage that I needed for what I was about to do. I knew that once I opened my mouth, there would be no turning back.

"Oh yeah?" Mark replied with that all-too-familiar cold yet questioning sideways glare. He took a swig of beer and set it back down on the table. "What would that be?"

Now whenever you got that sideways glare, you knew that the angry demons imprisoned deep within him were just waiting to be unleashed in order to wreak their havoc upon you in whatever way possible. I began to brace myself for the mighty blow, and mind you I definitely didn't take my eyes off of his arms; which were now folded across his chest. I needed to know exactly where those arms and hands were at all times. Have you ever watched an old western gunslinger movie? Notice how each foe will never take their eyes off their opponents, and always make sure to focus primarily on their hands? That was me. Always on the ready ... always trying to be the first to have a "successful draw." You needed to be the first to "draw" – and you needed to make sure that you darn well hit your target. If you weren't the first to make the move, or at least dodge the bullet, then you'd end up being the dead dude laying in the middle of the street. That's exactly how I felt each and every time I had to have a confrontation with Mark. I pressured myself to continue onwards. There's no turning back now! Just be ready!

"Well, a few weeks ago when I was at work I got a strange feeling. I felt like I was going to get sick. At first I thought that it was something I had eaten, but weirdly enough the sick feeling disappeared after about ten minutes or so. I thought nothing of it afterwards. That was until last week when I was at my Nana's."

"Yeah ... and? So what's your point?" That sideways glare deepened in intensity. Oh this isn't good ...

"My point is that when I was out home I took a test because my period never came. I was supposed to get it about two weeks ago. So I got scared and took a home pregnancy test. I tested positive. I'm pregnant."

"You're what?" Mark then unfolded his arms from his chest, sat forward in his chair, leaned menacingly across the table at me, and placed his hands on the table. "Say that again?"

"I'm pregnant."

KABAM!!!! As hard as I had tried to be prepared …
I wasn't. I just didn't react in time. Mark caught me
right square upside the head and knocked me flying
off my chair and into the fridge door behind me.

"Who's kid is it?" He screamed at me. "Who have
you been messing around with now?!"

"No one! I swear! I haven't been around anyone
but you! God I told you that before! Why don't you
ever believe me?"

"Well I don't know that with you going to work
all the time. Who knows who you've shacked up
with there at work! Get up! And quit your bawling
before you get another one!" He rearranged his chair
proper, sat back down, and started to nurse his beer
once more. Hmmm … something's slightly different
here. Those angry demons stopped their torture a
wee bit early on this time around. Yes, they were still
sitting out in the open ready to pounce once more,
but for the moment they had backed off. I guess this
man did have a conscious after all. He realized he
just hit a pregnant woman.

Badly shaken, head throbbing, and scared to
even move, I forced myself up off the floor. I righted
my chair and slowly sat back down, all the while
trying to stifle myself and my uncontrolled sobbing.
We sat there in silence, not daring to even look
at each other. It was Mark that finally broke that
silence: "Well. What are you going to do?"

"What do you mean what am I going to do?" I
wiped away the last of my tears and glanced over at
him nervously.

"I mean exactly what I said. What are you going to do? Either you're going to have an abortion or you're going to leave. I don't believe in adoption. So what's it gonna be?"

"I am NOT having an abortion!" I cried out defiantly. But that defiance was what set those demons off once more. They hated whenever I defied any of his requests or demands. In one quick motion Mark stood up and threw his half-full beer bottle at me. I ducked like a pro. HA! Missed me! But my triumph over that expert dodge was quickly squashed as he then overthrew the kitchen table on me. Hmph! So much for having a conscious I suppose. But with that final act he stormed out the door and made his way to the garage ... where we kept the Harley. Sure enough I hear it roar to life, shaking all the windows in the house. Then I breathed a huge sigh of relief as I heard Mark kick it into gear and tear off up the street. I knew then that I wouldn't see or hear tell of him for a number of hours.

However, I got quite the welcomed surprised. For the first time – and actually the only time ever – Mark did not return home. He stayed away for the night. So at least I got some sort of sleep into me. God knows I needed it.

So I had a bit of a reprieve from him. But when Mark returned the following night, that was a rather awkward hour. There were no beatings. In fact he didn't even speak a single word to me. He just went straight to bed. The following day, he was STILL drunk. And he continued to drink even then. He was

Lisa Caza

drunk for three days straight. In fact, Mark was so drunk that one afternoon he passed out hunched over sitting at our picnic table in the backyard. I was so amused at this that I actually took a picture of him. To this day I still have the picture ... somewhere. But in all seriousness, I really didn't know what troubled me more: the silent drunken state that he was in, or the state of limbo that I felt I was in. Something had to give way ... I knew it ... and it would be any moment. I was right.

The third day into his drinking binge Mark finally broke the silence by sneakily walking up behind me as I was washing dishes and gave me just one good solid punch on the back of the head. I saw stars that time. But at least that was the end of it. It was time for him to go to work. However, I guess that final blow to the head knocked some sense into me because the moment he left, that was the moment that I said to myself, "enough is enough."

I called into work sick that day. I had more important things to take care of. I started packing. I didn't have much to pack, but I didn't even know where I was going to go! All I knew was that I needed to leave: for my sake and for my unborn child's sake. I refused to lose another child.

I needed a break from packing, so I walked out into the backyard just to re-gather my thoughts and to try and figure out what to do. Just then, as if in answer to my prayers, a car pulled up into the driveway. It was a co-worker friend. She had finished her shift for the day and wanted to "check on me" as she knew something wasn't right. It wasn't normal for me to miss a day of work. She called out my name, and that's all I needed. I ran to her in my desperation and told her what happened.

"That's it. You're coming home with me. Right now. Get your things in the car and let's get out of here before he gets back."

And that's what I did. I went home with her. Upon my arrival I called my grandmother three thousand miles away and informed her of the goings on. She promised to send me the money for airfare once my cousin arrived home from holidays (as my cousin was power of attorney over her accounts). It was going to take two weeks. So there I stayed ... until I found myself in yet another lovely pickle of a predicament.

Chapter Six

Whoa. Okay. I have the belief to each their own – what people do in their private lives it's entirely up to them. But for pete sake don't try to get me involved!

Once again I found myself in a panicked state ... but in a very different situation. After a week of staying with my co-worker and her husband, they made it extremely clear to me that they had a very different lifestyle than what I was ever accustomed to (or even aware of for that matter. Remember by this time I am only nineteen years old – so I was still very naïve and inexperienced with life in general). They were nudists – which wasn't too bad. She was bisexual. That was okay too. And both of them were swingers. Yes, they frequently traded partners with other consenting couples. That was fine and dandy as well ... until they tried to put the moves on me.

Well I wanted no part of that! And in all honesty I was truly freaked out by it. Especially with the way that the husband would frequently make advances towards me ... and right in front of his wife. Not to mention one of them, I don't know who, would go into the guestroom where I was staying and make sure that there was a stockpile of pornographic magazines in plain sight ... obviously with the hopes of me picking them up, reading them, and getting turned on.

None of that worked. In fact, it just freaked me out more. It terrified me so much that again I found myself with the knowing that I had to get out of there ... and fast! But where do I go? What do I do? Who do I call? I don't have anyone else to rely on. Well I'll give you two guesses who I called, but I bet that you'll only need one.

I waited for the most opportune time: when the couple were both at work. It was noon, and I knew that Mark was working the afternoon shift. Therefore I still had a few hours. After wasting a full hour of humming and hawing, gathering up my courage, and ultimately swallowing my pride, I finally picked up the phone and dialed our phone number.

I have to be completely honest here and say that at this point I cannot remember all that was said in the conversation. All I do remember is telling Mark what was going on, and his panicked response:

"Oh my God. I'm getting you the hell out of there before they wind up raping you or something. I'm calling our neighbours to come get you and bring you home. Where are you?"

So in a nutshell that's what caused me to return to Mark. My neighbours raced over as fast as they could in their little beater of a car, packed up all my belongings again, and took me back home to him. But at this point I most certainly wasn't in the clear. We had the unfinished "business" of my pregnancy to deal with. However, I was in for a bit of a shock for when he came home from work and immediately addressed the issue with me (for obviously we couldn't continue without first addressing the situation). Mark cleared his throat and just dove in head first:

"I guess now you've passed the time limitation to have an abortion?"

"Yes I think so." Those four words literally took every ounce of strength I had in me ... and granted I hardly had any strength left to begin with after having gone through what I did that past month. All I could do was sit there silently. I couldn't move. I was paralyzed and totally unable to form even the most comprehensible of sentences. I sat ... and nervously waited ... and of course watched for that infamous sideways glare that signalled impending danger. Yet, it didn't appear. In fact, Mark felt to be rather calm ... sedated even ... in his energy and demeanor. All he did was let out one of the biggest sighs I've ever heard come from him. He looked up into the sky with a far-away look in his eye and whispered:

"Well, I suppose we're going to have a baby then."

Through the sheer shock and utter relief, my most immediate thought in that moment was, "Good for me. I won this battle." Yes indeed. I fought very bravely for my beliefs ... and most importantly for the beautiful blessing of a child that was growing inside of me. I had also kept my promise to myself and my first born child. I was going to have a baby.

Chapter Seven

*N*ine months later (yes I was overdue) I gave birth to a gorgeous and extremely healthy baby boy. My world revolved around that precious little man. You may laugh, but I wouldn't even set him down for a moment while I washed the dishes. No way! I held him in one arm while I washed dishes with the other. Needed to make a coffee, cook supper or vacuum the carpet? Not a problem! I just had to do it with one hand!

Throughout my pregnancy it was relatively happy and peaceful; we even had a close friend from home come out to visit us for a week. All I can remember about my pregnancy is a lot of joyous times ... and there was a closeness between Mark and I once more. It felt like we had returned to being the loving couple that we had become when we first moved out to Vancouver.

There was only one small episode of an angry outburst from Mark one night when he came home drunk from the bar. It was a rather strange episode actually. He rumbled into the garage on the Harley, put down the kickstand and turned it off. At that point I was standing at the back door to greet him. What he did next can only be described as just outright manic: he took one look at me, took his helmet off, and just threw it as hard as he possibly could. He threw it so forcefully that it rebounded off the cement almost like a basketball! What was strange is that for one, there was absolutely no forewarning. Not even the expression on his face tipped me off to what was about to occur. Secondly, to this day Mark doesn't even know why he did what he did. Needless to say I didn't want to stick around to find out what was wrong with him. So the moment I saw him hurl the helmet to the ground, I bolted through the house, ran through the front door in order to avoid him, and ran to my neighbour's. I stayed there the night just as a precaution (Mark didn't even come after me which I was quite grateful for). The following day he was extremely apologetic and quiet with me; he even took me out to supper that evening. Even though he never uttered the words "I'm sorry," I pretty much assumed that this was his way of doing so – that the supper was a form of a peace offering.

Other than that one episode, as mentioned life was quite peaceful and enjoyable. Mark absolutely adored and was quite proud of his new son. He would always comment at how handsome he was. He even developed this rather heart-warming behavior of needing to push our son in his stroller around in our backyard. Around and around he would walk, and with what I often would call a "perm-a-grin" on his face: a constant ear to ear smile. When our son was born, Mark had even insisted that he was to choose his first name. And when our son was just three months old, Mark bought a black lab puppy to grow up with him. At least I got to name him!

Although everything seemed like the "perfect family" to most outsiders, and indeed we seemed to be getting along rather well (as long as I did as I was told), there was still a dark ominous cloud hanging over us – of which only I could see.

By this time, Mark had changed ... and not for the better. He started to hang around with some members of quite the large biker gang, and with their guidance and support subsequently began to get involved in some of their illegal operations. As a result of this behavior, I was always on edge ... always worried about what I would do if the police ever came to bust Mark and his biker gang cronies.

Behind closed doors, Mark also developed a certain behavior with me that to this day makes me shudder (and this behavior would get worse as the years progressed). Almost every day that he was off work, he would demand that I dress in clothes that he specifically wanted me to wear. And 99.9% of the time the clothing was either see-through, skimpy or both. Mark managed to amass so many outfits (some of which he hacked up and made himself) that I had to put them all in two separate garbage bags! And yes ... I had to comply. You all must know what would happen if I didn't "obey the master." So for the most part, in order to avoid any of those consequences, I did as I was told. Mark would also place this horrible demand upon me whenever we were to go out for the night. Therefore it wasn't just in the privacy of our own home. It was also put upon me right in public. If I started to balk and whine about having to dress his way, he would threaten that we wouldn't go anywhere at all and stay home. And you're darn right that I would be embarrassed and self-conscious being out in public like that. I would always walk around with my arms folded in front of my chest, and never making direct eye contact. It was horrible. Even with Mark taking me to his favorite strip clubs didn't ease my discomfort. But, I complied to keep the peace ... whatever "peace" truly was.

Because Mark was doing so well financially (he had his regular job plus the nasty pot-growing operation), when our son was a year old we once again upgraded to quite the lovely bungalow rancher home in the outermost suburbs of Vancouver. I remember it had such an astoundingly beautiful view of the mountains from my living room window. I do believe that was the best house we ever lived in!

Chapter Eight

We remained in that mountain-view bungalow for three years. Over the course of those three years, I quietly kept to myself. I had no friends of my own; I merely focused on my son, as well as my growing psychic abilities that I finally realized weren't there just for me to amuse myself (but I had to keep that hidden from Mark because he didn't believe in psychic abilities at all. He would continuously make fun of me. And that's after the fact that I predicted that one of his friends was going to be seriously hurt in a motorcycle accident – which happened within just hours of my predicting it). Because I was always at home, I took it upon myself to enroll in a distance education course to become a veterinary technician. I graduated early, and with honors. However, when it came time for me to have an actual job interview with a local veterinary practice and then received a solid job offer from them, Mark made it known to me that he absolutely refused to take care of our son while I worked. He also made it very clear that he likewise did not want anyone else to take care of him. Today I believe those were just lame excuses. I believe the real reason behind those statements was that he just didn't want me working period. So unfortunately, my pursuit of my veterinary medicine diploma was a sheer waste of time (and money). Again I did as I was told: I denied the job offer and stayed at home "like a good girl."

Mark continued to be involved with the biker gang and their dealings. His alcohol and drug consumption massively escalated – to the point where he wasn't just drinking beer anymore; many times in came the good old whiskey, port, and tequila. Let it be known that hard alcohol did NOT "agree" with Mark at all. It turned him into someone (actually the better term to use here would be "something") that I didn't even recognize. The rage and completely erratic (and quite manic) behavior was phenomenally terrifying. Having been with Mark for eight years by this point, I had a pretty good idea what to expect from him from one moment to the next. But when he drank hard liquor, I couldn't predict a damn thing. What's so stupid is that Mark himself will to this day openly admit that he cannot handle "the hard stuff." So my question is why bother? Only he knows I suppose.

While during this period there were countless instances of alcohol-induced fits of rage, I have to admit that none of those fits were directly aimed towards me. At least not initially. There is only one night in particular that I specifically remember which caused me to flee the home with my one year old son in my arms. Mark came home from the bar (as usual) literally three sheets to the wind;

he obviously once again got his hands on the hard liquor. He was accompanied by his friend "Shorty" (who actually rented a room from us at the time). "Shorty" went straight to bed, while Mark took it upon himself to start swinging a wooden baseball bat at the chandelier in the dining room.

I was in bed when they first arrived, but upon hearing the commotion in the dining room of course dumb me had to go and investigate. One look into Mark's crazed wild eyes was enough for me to get the hell out of there. I raced down the hall, pounded on Shorty's door to wake him up, grabbed my son, and ran out the door to my neighbours. While I was there I paged Ralph, one of Mark's biker gang buddies, and he came right away to calm the situation down. Once everything was peaceful once more, Ralph assured me it was safe to return: Mark had passed out by that point at the dining room table, with dentures hanging halfway out of his mouth (that was always an amusing sight). However come the following morning, it seemed that Shorty actually received more damage than the chandelier. He could barely move, and was complaining that his back felt like it had been slammed by a truck. Upon investigating the backyard (as that's where Shorty and Mark wound up at some point duking it out), Mark found the wooden baseball bat broken right in half. And Shorty's back? You could see the very distinct swelling and marked outline of where the baseball bat made contact. Putting the pieces of evidence together, we all came to the conclusion that Mark broke the baseball bat across Shorty's back! That became the running joke between the two of them for years afterwards. But in all honesty, I really didn't find anything too funny about it.

From what I recall, after that incident with Shorty all was relatively quiet in terms of the fits of drunken rage. So long as I did as I was told, fulfilled all of Mark's insane demands unquestioningly, and didn't put up any fuss whatsoever ... all was well. The only thing that was occurring at this point was that Mark was trying to get me to join him in his drug use. I don't know how many times he would try to force me to take a drag off of a joint, eat a mushroom, or take some MDA. Thankfully Mark never lost his temper whenever I refused. He'd get frustrated, but never angry. However, he most certainly wouldn't give up on it either! He was incessant with his pushing it onto me. He would bother me so damn much that the odd time I would give in and take ONE tiny wee drag of a joint (which immediately made me ill). But one time he made me take something that he thought was MDA. That was THE BIGGEST mistake both Mark and I ever made. To this very day neither one of us know what it truly was; Mark called it horse tranquilizer. It may have well been considering what it did to me. It hit me while I was in, of all places, the bathroom. I called out to Mark to help me – for my legs didn't seem to want to work. Within a matter of minutes, I was completely incapacitated: I couldn't walk, I could barely talk, I was hallucinating like mad ... I even relived the horrifying moments of when I had to leave my first born baby at the hospital when it came time for my discharge. I remember screaming for my baby and trying to lunge off the couch that Mark had me pinned to (he had to almost sit on me to keep me there). I literally didn't know where or who I was. All Mark could do was cradle me in his arms. If I remember correctly I think that he was even praying (what?!) and kept saying how sorry he was for having made me do that.

Needless to say after that incident Mark never again tried to force me to take any harsh drugs. However, he still kept up with his pressing the joints onto me. He never did give up ... but at that point neither did I. I wanted no part of it ... and he knew it.

Chapter Nine

*J*ust as our son turned three years of age, Mark got slammed with some horrible news: he was once again getting laid off from work – and the layoff was permanent. As hard as he tried, he just couldn't find another job. Even Mark's dealings with the biker gang were suffering (thank god).

However, at this point our trusty old friend Shorty had moved to Alberta and had started his own home heating and air conditioning shop. Mark sat down with me and informed me of some 'new plans' that he had in his head:

"Shorty wants us to move out to Alberta. He said that he wants me to be his partner in his new company, and he even said that he is willing to sell us his house. I'll be making close to thirty dollars an hour!"

"Mark, I don't like this idea." By this time, my clairvoyant abilities were growing very quickly ... and strongly. The more I practiced and used my abilities, the stronger they became. By this time I'd have to say that my accuracy was already astoundingly high where 80% of my predictions would come true. "Seriously. I don't like this idea. It's not going to work out the way you think it will."

"What is wrong with you?" Mark immediately grew annoyed. I guess he had reason to? "Look. I can't get any work here! I've tried. Although we have some money saved up, pretty soon we're going to have a hard time paying the bills. I gotta do something. What else do you want me to do?"

"Yeah but ... I just have this strong feeling that we're going to get majorly screwed over and then we'll be in an even worse position. I wish you'd listen to me." I just couldn't let go of the images and messages I was hearing about this potential move. They weren't good ... and I felt the strongest sensation of impending doom I've ever felt. This time I wasn't frightened for myself. I was actually petrified ... for all three of us.

"Screw you and your feelings! We're going. End of discussion."

Chapter Ten

My prediction quickly became a horrible reality less than two months after moving out to Alberta. Mark worked horrendous hours at Shorty's home heating and air conditioning shop: twelve to fourteen hour shifts every day. Yet, he never saw a dime in wages. Not one dime. He was exhausted, and his love for and faith in our old friend was quickly turning into hatred and rage. To make matters worse, our so-called friend reneged on his promise to allow us to purchase his home. The ONLY good that came out of this particular situation is once again Mark and I became extremely close. He wouldn't even leave me in the house alone with Shorty. I believe that in this phase of our relationship, in looking back, THIS was the BEST our connection would EVER get. We came together as a true team; supporting each other the best we could.

The tension in the house that we shared with Shorty was so thick I could barely function (due to my increasing abilities and opening of my spirit and heart, even then I was very sensitive to negative energy ... and to this day I do the best I can to avoid being around it). Everything finally came to a head when Mark could stand it no longer and lashed out at our once good friend. Enough was enough! Where was his pay? We had continued to pay into the house (it was supposed to be a rent-to-own agreement) – including the monthly bills, we supported everyone's drinking and smoking habits, and even purchased all the groceries in the house. Now we're broke. Literally. At that moment we had a whopping twenty dollars in the bank ... all of our savings gone.

I cannot remember everything that was yelled between Mark and Shorty; I really didn't care back then because I had my own problem to worry about at the time: due to the eruption of all that negative energy, I wound up having a major asthma attack. That of course angered Mark even more. He raced to me with my inhaler in hand, put his arm around me to comfort me, and gently whispered:

"That's it. I've had it. Go get our son. We're going to my brother's. Right now. We're not staying here a second longer. Thank God we have Ma and my brother here. Let's go." It was those tender loving moments that truly renewed my love for that man. It's those moments that made me stay with him all that time (and beyond). Those moments made me forget all about the darkness ...

And indeed I agreed with him. We were *very* lucky to have both his mother and brother in the city to rely on. If it weren't for their support and help, I don't know what we would have done.

Anyways, he didn't have to tell me twice. I moved so damn fast I actually made it out to the truck with our son long before he even got there. That was just as well ... Mark and Shorty continued to yell and scream at each other for an additional few minutes. Again I don't know what was said between them – although whatever it was, it was nasty – because even years later Mark would curse Shorty and all that he had done to us. Very bad blood was created between two people who were, at one point, inseparable best buddies. And I didn't have the heart to tell him, "I told you so."

Chapter Eleven

$$\underset{}{\text{◈}}$$

W e stayed at Mark's brother's for approximately three weeks before Mark decided that he was going to travel back home to Ontario in order to find work and a home for us. Neither one of us liked the idea, but he had to leave me and our son with his brother while he attempted to venture out on this next quest. We just didn't have a choice. Or so we thought at the time ...

However, just days before Mark was scheduled to leave for Ontario, I found out that once again I was pregnant. What the hell was wrong with these birth control pills anyways? Never did I miss a pill, and I was actually on the strongest prescription the doctor could possibly give me. Yet still I got pregnant? Why?! And as you can imagine, yet again Mark threw at me that favorite old ultimatum of his:

"We can't have a baby now. Either you have an abortion or I'm out of here for good."

At this point I was so depressed and lost, I didn't know what to think, say or do anymore. Even I knew that it definitely wasn't a good time to have another baby! We had no money, no jobs ... need I mention we didn't even have a home? For once Mark was right. But I'd be damned if I was going to have an abortion. No way!

Well, I had to swallow my pride in this situation. I actually didn't even have the luxury of working with Mark's ultimatum. This time I literally had zero options available to me. Two days after I informed Mark of my pregnancy, I started hemorrhaging ... badly ... and it wasn't stopping. The flowing of blood was so heavy it actually sounded like I was urinating in the toilet. I screamed for Mark to come into the bathroom, and even he had the most worried look on his face. He was deathly afraid.

"You're going to the hospital. NOW!" With that said, he didn't hesitate a moment longer. He whisked me up into his arms and rushed me to the hospital emergency.

At the hospital, the doctors immediately took me in to the ultrasound to see what was going on. The look on the ultrasound technician's face told me that something definitely wasn't right. In fact, the situation was dire. But no one was telling me anything! Not one person said a single word! I remember the sheer panic that I felt as I waited in the hospital room. All I could say in my mind was, "What the hell is going on? Someone needs to tell me something ... anything ... just please stop this excruciating suspense and TELL ME! Are we both dying here or what? Why are they taking so long?! They had better pull their heads out of their arses and get in here ... NOW!" Finally, after an agonizing thirty minutes or so, a surgeon came in to speak to Mark and I together. I will never forget all that he said to us:

"I don't know how to explain this. I have never seen this before," the surgeon began. I found it disturbing that he couldn't keep eye contact with either Mark or I for very long. He constantly shifted back and forth between us and the medical folder he held in his hand. Nervously he continued, and with a distinct jittery quiver in his voice. "There are blood clots inside of your uterus that are actually pushing the placenta off the uterine wall. That's what is causing all of the hemorrhaging. According to the ultrasound you are eleven weeks along, and the baby itself is very healthy. But unfortunately, we will have to abort this pregnancy for the sake of your own health and well-being. Immediately. Quite frankly, I don't even know how you managed to get this far along."

The room started to spin. From that moment on I couldn't hear any further discussions, see anything, or even focus my thoughts proper. All I could hear were the words, 'have to abort this pregnancy' echoing in my head. I was in a total state of shock and disbelief. But then ... then I felt a rage and deep resentment within myself that I have never felt before. I remember my exact thoughts: "WHY?! Why God did you make me pregnant and then make me have to go through this horrible procedure? WHY?! Now Mark gets what he wants ... I bet he's just tickled pink now."

The following morning I was admitted into the hospital and they carried out the procedure. One thing to note: I forced Mark to stay by my side throughout the entire thing. He wanted me to go through this how many times? Well ... now he can sit there and watch. And yes ... yes he did stay. He stayed for the entire procedure (and apparently held my hand throughout). I personally don't remember anything about the procedure itself (because they knew my emotional state and attitude towards what was about to occur, they sedated me and gave me a memory block in an IV). But I don't think Mark wasn't too impressed by what he saw and heard. Good! That was my full intention. I had the hope that it had scarred him for life.

Chapter Twelve

⁓

*T*he day after I had the procedure done, Mark left to begin his journey back home to Ontario ... leaving our son and I in the care of his brother.

Staying at his long-time friend Edward's place, it didn't take Mark long to find work. Yet our son and I still couldn't join him as of course we still needed a home. The thing is, the longer that I remained separated from Mark, the more my anxiety grew ... I don't know why but I just had the sneaky suspicion that Mark might sleep around on me (funny how that one works huh? As you may recall, Mark loved to falsely accuse me of being unfaithful to him.).

While I absolutely adored Mark's brother with all my heart and spirit and loved spending time with him, I just couldn't stay separated from Mark any longer. My anxiety levels just grew the more that time went on.

Eventually my anxiety got the best of me and I made a phone call to my grandmother. I didn't tell her the whole truth of the situation and how high my anxiety was (she was always the worrier and didn't like to hear anything wrong on my end); I just simply let on to her that I couldn't handle being away from Mark any longer. Being her natural unconditionally loving, generous, and understanding self, she immediately sent me the money for the airfare. Within two weeks my son and I were reunited with Mark.

Because we didn't have a home of our own, my son and I stayed with my grandmother while Mark continued to keep a room with his old buddy Edward. Mark worked through the week, and on weekends he would come to stay with us at my grandmother's. By this time we started searching for a home more avidly; we hated having to be apart all week, we hated living in the city, and we yearned to have some privacy. And this time we wanted to buy our own home. We definitely had enough of having to pay someone else's mortgage!

We finally found a three bedroom, two-story home that was within our price range, located in what's considered cottage country. It was a beautiful area full of wildlife, farm land, and even a huge lake a block away where we could take our son swimming. However, because we didn't quite have enough for a down payment, my grandmother gave us a helping hand ... and we sold the Harley. We hated having to do that; but like I said to Mark, "The three of us can't live on a bike." For once he agreed with me, but you could see that selling the bike took a huge chunk out of his heart.

This house represented a brand new start for us. It was to be built from the ground up. The first time we saw our home, it was literally just a hole in the ground (they were just about to pour the foundation). I was so excited, as I was allowed to choose all the building materials: slate grey bricks, light grey siding, black shingles, a very light beige carpet, a country rose floral pattern for the flooring/tiles, dark cherry wood kitchen cupboards and grey marble counter tops. I called it my "mini castle." For once Mark actually had nothing to say! He gave me full control over how the house was going to look. It was such a fulfilling and thrilling experience for me ... yet it likewise felt very odd to me simply because I wasn't used to having ANY amount of control ... over anything. Mark usually held the controlling reins on every imaginable thing. Looking back on this, I would have to say that perhaps Mark felt the need to allow me some control considering if it weren't for my grandmother then we wouldn't have had the home at all. At least that's my understanding at this point.

Within two months my "mini castle" was completely finished and we were able to move in. At first we didn't have one single piece of furniture, so our son thought it was the coolest thing ever to be able to eat, sit, and sleep on the newly carpeted living room floor. Everything had that new smell to it ... but so much so that it actually caused me to have the absolute worst migraine headache I ever had. I didn't care. It was the summer of 1997. I had my three year old son, and I had been with Mark for a little over eight years. And I felt like I was on top of the world. We had our new home, our fresh new start ... and all was well.

Chapter Thirteen

ow. I'm not fanatically superstitious, but how ironic is it that we have now reached chapter *thirteen* of this book ... and this is where unfortunately my life took yet another horribly dark turn for the worst. And this was a turn that I never pulled out of ... at least not with Mark. It all goes downhill from here ... and fast. To be quite honest with you, this is where my brain wants to go in a thousand different directions all at once. I don't know where to begin. So much happened from here on in. I suppose I shall begin with the *last* happy moment I ever experienced in my relationship with Mark. Therefore with that said, let's look at chapter thirteen as the "calm before the storm."

November, 1997 – three months after the deaths of both my grandfather and the beautiful Lady Diana (both passed away on the same day – August 31) and four months after moving into our new home, I find myself sweating bullets once more. I hadn't felt this profound fear and horridly sinister energy since I found out I was pregnant with my son: impending doom ... heartache ... *chaos*. Mark handed me the box that contained the two home pregnancy tests (I always bought two because of course I just could never accept the first answer. I always had to try and prove it wrong with the second test).

"Well go and do it. We're not going to know unless you take the test ... dummy."

I gathered up the tests and my courage. Slowly I got up ... my legs ... they felt like jello. Not once making direct eye contact with Mark, I made darn sure that I gave him quite the wide girth as I nervously walked past him. I could barely take those few steps to the bathroom. Mark knew how petrified I was, and I don't know if he took pleasure in that or not. I'm still trying to answer that, but the spiritual side of me would like to hope not.

I took the first test. The result showed up *immediately*. There was no waiting for it to make a decision. It was instant. Knowing that this was rather odd, right away I took the second test the best I could. Same thing. Same result. And the result was instantaneous. I was pregnant ... AGAIN! For the result to have shown up so rapidly I thought to myself, "Good Lord I must be extremely pregnant for that to happen."

The room started to spin and my heart started to pound in my ears ... AGAIN! I try to calm myself best I could and made my way back to where Mark was. When I sat down, a very new energy and attitude washed over me: angry determination mixed with resentment. I turned and glared at Mark. There was definite eye contact there wow!

"So what's it going to be this time, Mark? Abortion, adoption, or are you going to leave me? Which is it?" I couldn't control the rage welling up inside of me. I hissed those words at him with such a venomous force, but I don't think he even noticed how hateful my energy was. He looked over at me with a small grin and gave a slight chuckle. What he said next sent me over the edge:

"Well, I guess our son loses his play room. I knew that we were going to have another kid at some point eventually anyways." With that having been said, I immediately broke down into tears; tears of profound relief, glorious happiness, and utter shock. All Mark could do was chuckle.

Fast-forward two weeks later, I found myself laying on the ultrasound bed to find out how far along I was in my pregnancy, and to ensure that the baby was healthy and thriving. The technician was going through the regular routine actions that I had grown so familiar with: checking the placenta, taking measurements, and so on. Then she asked me one of the routine questions that I've been asked before:

"Are there any sets of twins on either side of the family?"

"Nope! None." Wait a second. The look on that woman's face just didn't feel right to me. Something was definitely different about this supposed routine question. I had to ask, "Why?"

The technician slowly turned the ultrasound monitor around so that I could see it. She gave me the widest possible grin and said,

"Well ... because there's baby number one," she pointed to a small, indescribable blob on the left side of the monitor, and then pointed to another peanut-looking blob on the right but slightly lower, "And there's baby number two. Congratulations! You're having twins my dear."

"Aw hell. So that's why the pregnancy test result showed up so quickly...Now whaa.."

Pooof! The room goes black. Oh oh. Dear Lisa fell into total oblivion.

———~~~◦◦◦◦◦◦~~~———

An hour later, I sat down at my Nana's kitchen table, poured myself a cup of tea, and looked at her somberly. I could tell that she wasn't too overly impressed. Actually she was worried to death about me. But of course she would never outwardly express her dissatisfaction or upset to me. All she wanted was for me to be happy. My entire life she would always do whatever it was in her power to make sure I was happy and taken care of. God how I love that woman. She was my rock.

"So how did it go at the ultrasound?"

"Oh it was just freaking ducky, Nana." She didn't like me cursing – it wasn't very lady-like after all. She would always say that it wasn't how she had raised me; that I was a 'proper lady' with 'proper English manners.' But in this particular case she didn't chastise me at all. "Sorry Nana. It didn't go well."

"Well what happened?" My grandmother pressed on. "You're not going to have twins are you?"

Right then I couldn't help it ... I choked on my tea. No joke. Tea literally came spewing out my nose and mouth, spattering all over my Nana's delicate white lace tablecloth. Great ... I just ruined a seventy year-old tablecloth. I swear to you all right here and now on all that is good and divine: those were the *exact words* that she said to me. But ... how in the *hell* did she know this?! No one else knew other than myself and my doctor. And she said it so matter-of-factly ... like there was absolutely no reason why I wouldn't have twins. It was almost like ... well ... like she was fully expecting it at some point.

I knew right then and there that this was obviously where I inherited my own psychic abilities. They came from my Nana! In those few moments, through my choking and trying to regain my composure, a number of questions then started to swirl about in my mind: Why didn't she tell me before? Why didn't she foster me with my abilities? Why did she always 'shush me' when I tried to tell her certain feelings and predictions that I was picking up on (like when I predicted the F4 tornado when I was eleven)? I know the answers to those questions now. But back then I wasn't as learned in the metaphysical field – I didn't understand that in her day it was *never* discussed. In fact, such things as psychic abilities, mediumship, tarot cards, and so on were considered 'evil' and taboo. My poor Nana was still caught up slightly in that way of thinking. She was fearful of letting on to others – including me – about her own clairvoyant ability.

I helped my Nana clear off the tea spattered tablecloth. She was totally silent ... I know she was waiting for my answer. Although it was quite obvious by my reaction, she knew what my answer was. She just wanted to hear it come out of my own mouth. I had no choice. I had to admit she was dead bang on the money.

"I don't know how you know, but yes. They said that I'm carrying twins. I'm only five weeks along though." Like she totally wasn't expecting it, my Nana's jaw dropped to the floor in seemingly pure shock. While that was indeed her usual reaction when she was shocked, disgusted, or surprised about something, I think this time around it was just an act for my sake. As if! She predicted I was going to have twins and then she acts shocked? No Nana you didn't fool me. Not this time.

"Good Heavens! What are you going to do?"

"It isn't really a question of what I am going to do," I think that was the *only* time in my entire life that I spoke so sternly to my beloved grandmother. "It's mainly a question of what Mark is going to do."

——◦◦◦◦◦◦◦◦——

With shaking hands I picked up my Nana's old rotary phone and dialed Mark's work number. Yeah ... he wasn't going to like this tidbit of news. Sure, he was fine with me being pregnant. But he most certainly didn't sign up for having two babies at once. I was so sure that he was going to flip right out. That old familiar feeling of dread and utter terror began to wash over me as the phone on the other end started to ring. The receptionist answered and I requested to speak to Mark. After an agonizingly long minute Mark finally picked up.

"So how did it go?" Mark sounded unusually happy and bouncy. In realizing his awesome mood, I broke down into tears right away. I don't know why his happy-go-lucky energy made me shatter. Perhaps I was so concerned about ruining his day? Well, I had to follow through. He had to know.

"We're having twins." I just blurted it out. The thing is though, it didn't come out proper. Through my uncontrollable sobbing (I was almost hyperventilating at this point), it sounded more like 'we're brble brble ble.' So of course Mark didn't understand a single word. He gave a slight giggle and tried to calm me down.

"What?" he laughed. "Stop crying. I can't understand you. Especially with the punch press going on here in the background. Take a deep breath and try again." I helplessly glanced over at my grandmother silently sitting beside me. She merely nodded her head at me in encouragement and weakly smiled. I did as I was told ... with my tears more under control I tried it again.

"We're having twins."

"You're joking!" Mark began to laugh. He actually didn't believe me.

"I'm dead serious. They said we're having twins." The tears started to flow once more, and the blubbering words started to come out of my mouth again. I don't know if Mark understood or heard what I said next. "What are we going to do?"

But Mark couldn't answer me even if he did understand my question. He was too busy laughing. He was laughing so hard that now *he* was the one that couldn't breathe. Maniacal laughter, hacking and choking ... that's all I heard on the other line.

———～w•๑๛๏๛●๑•w———

Two weeks before my actual due date of August 31, 1998, and after almost a week of being in labor (the doctor said that multiple birth labors were prolonged ... he wasn't kidding!); I gave birth to two absolutely gorgeous baby girls. I *forced* Mark to stay with me throughout the entire labor and delivery (because he refused to be there for our son, and hadn't even been present for his other two sons from his previous marriage). He tried to sneak away, but my doctor and two nurses caught him. Ha! The doctor even put Mark on the spot and made him cut both of the girls' umbilical cords. After I had delivered both girls and the doctor was busy doing whatever business he was doing down there in my area, I happened to look up at Mark to see what he was doing. What I saw I never thought would ever happen. Not in a million years: he was holding a baby in each arm, looking down at them proudly ... and what was that? THE MAN WAS CRYING! What? At first I was shocked, but then my exhaustion and sheer frustration with all that he had done to me in the past washed over me. What I said to him in that moment wasn't the nicest of things:

"What are *you* crying about? For God sake *I'm* the one that just gave birth!" While all the nurses and my doctor thought it quite amusing, I don't think Mark even heard me. He was in his own little 'daddy world.'

Back in my hospital room, I realized quite a bit of time passed. Where was Mark? Not even my nurse knew. So she called the nursery to follow up. Sure enough, he was there. Apparently he took his time selecting little sleepers for the babies, he bathed them and dressed them. The nursery nurse had to shoo him out of there and back to me. What a man. He confused me ... but in a good way this time.

Refusing to rest before seeing my newborn baby girls, Mark plopped me down into a wheelchair and ushered me straight to the nursery. The heavy red curtains were drawn across the nursery's large picture window. It was as if the hospital staff were so proud of these babies they had to create something of a wee show for me (they actually were proud as their birth gave them national publicity – which is another story. I'll keep you in suspense ha!). Slowly they opened the curtains to reveal my beautiful angels. My eyes immediately fell upon my second little girl ... I couldn't help it ... I started wailing. The tears streamed down my face like a raging waterfall. That baby girl was a spitting image of my first born daughter: full head of thick shoulder-length dark auburn hair, round chubby face, even her wee little toes were the same. Mark knew immediately what was going on.

"Shit!" Mark muttered as he hastily spun me around and wheeled me back to my room. "Sorry hon. I should have prepared you." Yeah ... too bloody late now. Arsehole!

However, that was actually quite the massive spiritual awakening for me. I began to ponder over all that I had gone through with my first child and my miscarriage-slash-abortion. I also came to realize that the twins' actual due date was literally a year to the day that my grandfather (and Lady Diana) passed away. Could it be? Yes it could! I came to the solid conclusion that those two baby girls were true gifts from Divine. Divine was trying to return to me what I had perceived as having lost. I 'lost' two girls (well, the second loss of course we didn't know for sure if it was a girl or not ... but I strongly felt that it had been) ... so I was receiving two girls in return. They were true divine blessings that I cherish with all my heart and soul. I never felt such tremendous joy as what I did when those girls were born. However, that joy was not long-lived.

Chapter Fourteen

*A*s I had mentioned at the beginning of the last chapter, the birth of my twin girls was literally *the last* happy moment that I experienced throughout the remainder of my relationship with Mark. Even Mark's long-awaited marriage proposal (which took place when the twins were a year old) wasn't all that joyous.

"You want to get married?" Mark announced out of the blue. All I could do was sit there in silent shock and stare at him like he was from another planet. "Well, we have a company Christmas party next week. We'll go to city hall and then to the Christmas party afterwards. So you have a week to get ready. Deal?"

Wasn't that the most romantic proposal you ever heard? At this point we were together for nine years. And that's all I got? Was I disappointed you ask? Well ... even as I write this I have just one phrase repeating over and over in my mind: "Hick! What a hick!" How's that for disappointment? Yuck! It certainly wasn't the wedding that I had always dreamed of that's for sure. Despite Mark's sheer lack of passion and romance ... and despite the continued infrequent bouts of abuse at Mark's hand ... I agreed. Thus so was my first wedding: a rushed shot-gun style city hall extravaganza (yeah right). The only family and friends in attendance were the judge, Mark's son and his girlfriend (who was my witness because I had no friends ha ha!), and Mark's witness. No wedding cake. No photographers. No white dress or veil. No reception. No honeymoon planned. It's a wonder we even had wedding rings for pete sake. Oh! Oh! We did have flowers though! Of course I didn't know what I was doing ... and I was rushing ... but I made sure we all had flowers ... including the bridal bouquet. They were expensive ... more expensive than my dress. But that's because they were real. Ha! I guess I never heard of FAKE flowers ... they would have been more appropriate and fitting for the occasion that's for sure.

Our wedding was a joke, and all I could feel throughout was disappointment ... and despair at the fact that my grandmother, cousins and brother couldn't even be there for me on that day.

Chapter Fifteen

*A*t this point here dear readers, I truly don't know how to proceed. My life and experience with Mark was so chaotic after the birth of my girls ... so many things were said and done ... I can't even put a chronological order to everything. I'm quite impressed with myself and how great I've done up until this point. But now, everything is all jumbled and mixed up. Of course I distinctly remember events ... some of them (you need to understand that with many folks who go through traumatic experiences, some memories become blocked from their consciousness.). The problem is I can't pinpoint exactly when each event occurred from here on in. There's just way too much.

As a result of my dilemma here, unfortunately I'm going to have to change up the formatting of this book. Just to get through the remaining few years. The best (and only) way I can get through this is to basically list each occurrence/event as it comes to the forefront of my mind. Each 'event' will act as its own 'mini section' in this chapter.

I will also take this opportunity to apologize in advance for the dark nature of the remaining contents of this chapter. There's not a whole lot I can do about that; everyone who knows me knows full well that I am far from being a dark and dreary person. In fact today, I'm quite the opposite. Nor am I trying to 'pick on' my ex-husband by only focusing on the negative. Sure there were certainly days here and there where I found myself laughing or was happy. However, those days were few and far between. It's just how my life was back then. There were hardly, if any, happy moments to divulge to you. I'm so sorry. I truly am. But the following 'mini chapters' make up the cold harsh truth of only a miniscule amount of what I endured.

───~w○○℮ɤ○○ɤℓ○○w───

I haven't brought this up as it wasn't really relevant to the main story until now, but throughout my entire relationship with Mark I suffered from horrible teeth problems. When I was twelve years old, my mother decided it wise to make me get braces. To make a very long story short, I was to have the braces on for only two years. I had them on for a little over *four* years; without regular dental cleanings or maintenance. For the last year of having them on, the braces actually went completely unchecked by any orthodontist or dentist. With me being a child, I had no means to get to a dentist let alone the money to pay for it! It wasn't until I was sixteen when a friend of mine had enough and said they were going to pay for them to be removed. Well ... the damage by that time had been done. The braces (and build-up of plaque) had eaten away at ... and horribly stained ... the majority of my teeth. I had no money to fix them. Then later, after having gone through three full-term pregnancies, my teeth suffered even more devastating damage. So that's a wee bit of history to lead up to my main point ...

Mark received medical and dental benefits at his place of employment. I was absolutely ecstatic! All I could think about was how I could finally get these horribly nasty teeth fixed. I would be able to smile again! I was so thrilled I made an appointment with the dentist as soon as I knew the benefits had kicked in (the only way I knew they were active was when Mark went to get some new upper dentures).

I go to the dentist, get x-rays, a deep cleaning and a treatment plan. I was so eager to begin I booked my first treatment appointment a mere three days later. Just as I was about to walk out the office door, the receptionist called out to me:

"Wait! Lisa, you have to give me your payment for the work done today." Huh? What payment? What the hell was this crazy woman talking about? My husband has benefits!

"No," I replied sternly. For some reason, I was actually becoming rather angry with this woman. "My husband has benefits through his work. His insurance information should be on file there." After a few moments of searching her computer's database, it was clear that she was coming up dry.

"I'm sorry," the receptionist slowly shook her head. "But the only person listed on this gentleman's insurance benefits is him. I don't see your name here anywhere Lisa."

Needless to say, to shorten the story and get right to the point, that 'gentleman' did not list me, our son or our girls on his benefits! I was fuming! I was so angry I couldn't even think straight, and I was stuck with a $300 dentist bill that I couldn't even pay because the prick wouldn't let me work! What did I do? I called my grandmother right there from the dentist's office and told her what was happening. That poor receptionist; I could see that she was close to tears she felt so horrible for me. But yet once again my grandmother came to my rescue; she immediately got my cousin to call into the dentist's and pay them with her credit card – which my grandmother reimbursed her for.

So much for getting my teeth fixed. More on that dilemma much later ...

———ᘉᘉᖁᖁᘉᘉ———

In April of 2000 my world was suddenly and quite literally shattered when my beloved grandmother passed away. To add insult to injury, a mere three days later our dearest and longest friend Edward (the friend Mark stayed with when we first moved back to Ontario), was killed in a tragic car accident. The grief that both Mark and I experienced was profound. I cannot describe Mark's grief for that was his experience, but for me I was close to suicidal. It took every ounce of strength in me to not kick that four-barrel in on my Camaro and slam head-first into an oncoming transport truck. The only thought that saved me was that of my three children at home: my then six year old son and two year old twin girls. It got to a point where Mark was so nervous of me driving that a few times he took my car keys and hid them on me. That was about the *only* good thing he had done for me in these latter years.

I didn't want it – I just wanted my Nana back, but I received a handsome inheritance upon her death. Other than my mother, I was the only other beneficiary in my grandmother's will. I received a total of just over $75,000; With Nana's verbal stipulation that I create a bank account solely in my name – and one that Mark could not access.

My Nana was very smart ... but she obviously didn't realize the true scope of Mark's domineering and controlling ways. He still managed to get his hands on it – and it was through sheer brute force.

Mark took it upon himself to make me pay off both of his credit cards (which was a combined total of $7,000). He made me pay the entire bill for an addition that we put on the back of our house (which was another $13,000). He even decided that he should quit working! He didn't work for over a year ... that's right ... he waited until all of my money was gone. But just before all my money sadly disappeared – there was one major purchase that I so desperately needed to make happen:

I bought Edward's 1989 Custom Harley from his widow for $18,000. Edward's son expressed interest in having it, but both Mark and I held the attitude that if anyone should get that bike then it needed to be us. Not only had Mark known Edward since he was thirteen years old, Edward's son didn't even know how to ride or take care of a motorcycle.

I want you all to remember the Harley, for it comes into play once again relatively shortly.

———— ᴡᴡᴏᴏᴇᴛᴏᴏᴛᴇᴏᴏᴡᴡ ————

As you may remember from earlier on, Mark had developed this extremely annoying ... well ... I guess fetish ... of forcing me to only wear clothes that he wanted me to wear; clothes that were *always* see-through and skimpy. Well, this 'fetish' became a thousand times worse as the years progressed – to the point where it was almost a daily occurrence. He didn't care if we had company over, if we were out in public, if our three children saw it ... in his warped mind he saw absolutely nothing wrong with it. To add further to this though, Mark also would try to force me to exotic dance for him – and a few select friends of his choosing. To this day if one were able to confront and ask his spirit about it he'd readily admit to it, but he would add the comment that I ... me ... Lisa ... loved it. That was Mark's warped thinking at work.

For the dratted record: *no I did not love it.* In fact, over the years I grew increasingly frustrated and sickened by it. I had even grown the courage to try and fight against him about it. Constantly repeating myself, saying: "Mark! No! I don't want to. Mark, I said no!" I would 'win' the battle maybe half of the time ... but only because Mark would drunkenly pass out before he even got the chance to verbally give up.

———∿∿◦◦⌒⊙⌒⊙⌒◦◦∿∿———

When Mark turned fifty ...

All I can say at this point? He turned into a complete stranger to me. I didn't know him anymore. I don't know what happened inside of him, but it was like someone just suddenly flipped a switch inside his brain that went from 'half-assed sane' to 'totally psychotic.' Part of me would like to believe that it was the male version of menopause that was affecting him. And sure that would explain maybe a few things. However, it most certainly didn't explain *everything.*

The 'man-o-pause' as I call it likely caused his new infatuation with cocaine. It also likely would explain his difficulty in getting or maintaining an erection (then again alcohol did that to him as well quite often – and he was drinking every other day by this point ... drunk every weekend for sure). Even Mark taking more chances drinking and driving could be possibly explained by this 'man-o-pause.' However, I just cannot see the logic behind it having caused Mark to push other men onto me and try to flaunt me around in front of them – almost like he was advertising me. The 'other men' that were 'lucky enough' to be allowed by Mark to touch me would be select friends. I don't know how many times I shooed off the other men/friends of Mark's. Not one of them got too close. The moment they just barely touched me or brushed up against me I would violently shove them away and tell them to 'f-k off.' I even recall threatening one of Mark's friends in particular: the guy was married! So I used that against him. If he were to even *think* of touching me *ever* again, I would go straight to his wife and tell her. Then she'd deal with him!

—————

Mark's fathering skills were not the greatest (and would prove to be next to nil as you'll see in a bit) by this point. Whenever he was home during the day, all Mark did was sleep on the couch and watch a sport or the news on television. He never spent time with our son or two girls. In fact, all three of them learned very quickly that whenever their father was home they needed to be extra quiet otherwise he'd 'get mad.' If they even became minutely audible to him, and he didn't like it, he wouldn't nicely tell them to tone things down. He'd just yell, "Shut up!" or "Be quiet!" Mark had absolutely no interest in the children; unless it was to put on a show for my visiting brother or neighbours. However, Mark believed right up until his passing that he was a good father. I'm sorry but a good father includes more than that of brushing and braiding a four-year old girl's hair after her evening bath. If asked today, neither of my girls even recall him having done that. All they remember is being yelled at to be quiet and to clean up their mess of toys. My son has also re-told a story of his own where Mark punched him in the face while he lay in his bed one night; all because he hadn't cleaned up his room earlier that day. I confronted Mark about that many years after we separated, and he of course flat-out denied having ever touched our son.

———— ᴡᴡᴏᴏᴏᴏᴏᴏᴏᴡᴡ ————

Mark's new 'angry outburst fad' was that of coming home drunk and complaining to me about how we never had any money, that he was sick and tired of supporting me and the kids, and that I needed to get a real job. I made the mistake one night of countering back at him:

"Well Mark maybe if you didn't piss it away every day, didn't shove it up your nose whenever you get the chance, and allowed me to get a real job, then maybe we *would* have more money!"

"How *dare* you pin that all on me you stupid witch!" he snarled menacingly (and he didn't actually use the word 'witch' – it was something much, much worse – another quite colorful four-letter word). "What kind of job could you ever get? McDonald's? Hey! Anyone want a burger?"

ZING! SMASH! Wheee! There goes another beer bottle hurling through the air and headed straight towards me. I'd become so 'pro' at ducking fists and bottles over the years that it actually became a finely tuned skill or art rather than sheer reflex. And yes, of course that would send Mark into a totally new level of rage. At times I didn't know what was worse: Mark's raging, pounding fists or the magic flying beer bottles. I suppose it's one of those things where I just had to pick my poison: which one would I prefer today? I didn't much like the choices ...

———~∿∿◦◦◦◦❀◦◦◦∿∿———

I must take a few moments here to explain to you that since the conception of my twin girls (I had mentioned in chapter thirteen about my insight regarding the girls and how divine had clearly intervened in my life – that's when I really started to plunge forward along my spiritual path), I had begun a path of spiritual truth-seeking. As a result of my pursuit for enlightenment and divine wisdom, my psychic abilities grew exponentially – to the point where I wasn't just using my 'three c's' as I called them (clairvoyance, clairaudience and clairsentience – which I have had and thus used since I was a very young child). I was also starting to receive images for predictions of the future, I was beginning to communicate with my spirit guides (as well as other people's guides), and even began to feel the 'stirrings' of a mediumship ability (so in other words I could sense spirits around but I couldn't communicate with them in any way).

So, as a result of Mark constantly whining and complaining about not having enough money, and hounding me about not having a 'real job,' I finally started listening to a number of divine signs that I was receiving for the last year: I applied to, and was successfully hired for, my very first 'position' with quite the large online psychic hotline. While I had been reading for others for many years prior to this (of course always behind Mark's back), this was actually my very first opportunity to become available on a more global scale. It was all very new to me: under obvious time limits I needed to provide psychic insight and guidance to clients via live, online chat. At first I felt quite intimidated, but once I realized how accurate my readings were and how all the clients who came to me adored me and actually highly valued my insight, I quickly overcame my nervousness and ultimately looked forward to every shift. I believed that I finally found my intended purpose on this planet. I felt needed, respected, and fulfilled ... which was something that I hadn't ever had the pleasure of feeling before.

No longer could I keep my psychic work hidden from Mark; not when I had this new online job. Because I became one of their most requested readers, I needed to be available online most evenings and weekends ... therefore Mark certainly knew what I was doing. And he definitely made sure that I was clearly aware of how he felt about psychics and ANYTHING to do with metaphysics and the paranormal. There were many times I would be actively chatting with a client when he would make the stupidest comments:

"Ha ha so you got another sucker roped in do ya?" Mark would chuckle from the couch behind me. "Tell them to expect a bolt of lightning!" He'd then burst into the most hysterical fits of laughter. Mark was the type of individual who always laughed at his own jokes ... no matter how disrespectful, nonsensical, or crude they may be. All I could do was shake my head in disgust and just try to keep on going with the readings.

Due to Mark's complete lack of respect for the work that I did, he even caused me to lose clients. There were countless times when the telephone would ring or one of the children needed something. Would he get himself up off of that couch to respond to the incessant phone rings or demanding of the kids? Nope! This is what would happen instead:

"The phone's ringing," Mark would inform me ... like I'm deaf and can't hear the bloody thing. "Are you going to answer that or what?"

"I'm busy! Can't you see that? Can't you get it? You're just sitting there!" I would be so frustrated and resentful that I'd lose my entire focus in the reading. And because I'd be too busy dealing with Mark's ignorance, I'd of course forget to type. So POOF! There goes another client lost.

"You and your scamming and those suckers are no different. Fine. Stay there. Don't get up. I'll get it." Of course by that time the phone would have stopped ringing, and the kids would have found something else to amuse themselves with while they waited for one of us.

"Great. Now you get up? After I lose another poor soul who needed my help. I'm trying to work. I can't work when you don't help me out just a tiny wee bit here. And by the way I don't care what you say about me anymore. But when it comes to others, they are NOT suckers! They genuinely need guidance and that's what I'm there to provide them with. You also need to remember what I'm trying to do here.

If you can't accept the fact that I'm trying to help others, then can you at least remember why I got this position in the first place? You complain all the time about us never having money. So I got this job to help."

"F-off!" That was always Mark's favorite response to something he actually didn't have an intelligent argument for. "Get a real job."

Here we go again. I guess that wasn't a real job???? Oh well ... the job didn't last long anyways because only a mere two months after I started on that website, Mark took it upon himself to smash my entire computer system in one of his fits of rage – thus rendering me completely inoperable ... and jobless once more. I was heartbroken. Just when I found one of my true purposes for this incarnation and felt so useful! What took me ten years to find, he essentially took away from me in a matter of ten seconds.

———⁓⁓∘◦◖◗◖◗◦∘⁓⁓———

This is the last 'mini-chapter' because to be completely honest with you, all I would be doing is repeating myself. Every few days there would be something that I'd need to deal with when it came to Mark. Whether it was an angry outburst and beating, fulfilling outrageous demands, dealing with constant alcohol and drug abuse, pushing away the men that Mark would try to shove onto me (yet he would make absolutely horrifying comments regarding my physical body. On one occasion he likened my breasts to that of a couple of fried eggs.

It was extremely hurtful to me, but he thought it was the best joke he ever came up with) – or whatever else. The emotional and physical abuse by this point was virtually constant.

I fully believe the reason why the abuse escalated so much in the last two years was because over the course of the first thirteen years of being with Mark I matured tremendously. He didn't like the change in me ... he saw that he was slowly beginning to lose control as I started to fight against him more often than what I would comply. It angered him even more; therefore he would lash out more frequently and harshly. He was trying to re-assert his power over me.

Frankly, the death of my beloved grandmother was a major pivotal moment in my life: it permanently (and drastically) changed me. It forced me to grow up ... and wisen up. As a result of all my growth and change, I started to actually abhor Mark. When I say abhor – I mean it. I got to the point where I was thoroughly disgusted with him. I cringed at the thought of him even touching me; I'd get sick to my stomach whenever he tried to drunkenly hug or kiss me ... and I would frequently pretend that I was fast asleep when he tried his sexual advances (which never worked by the way as he actually didn't care if I was asleep or not). I became resentful for all that he had taken away from me: my self-esteem, my personal power, my dignity (not to mention the more physical losses: my first-born child, my horses, my career path). I desired to have more power and control over my life, and began to use my mouth more by speaking up and out about certain things I did not like or agree with. This isn't a very nice statement to make, but there were many nights I'd be lying in bed waiting for Mark to return home from the bar ... I knew exactly what to expect when he arrived: either he was going to be all touchy-feely or a raging lunatic. Either way I wasn't looking forward to it. So I would wish and pray with all my heart and with tears streaming down my face ... that he would end up getting killed in an accident so that I would no longer have to deal with him. I would then be free! However, that wish was never granted.

That's the trouble though: I was waiting for someone or something to rescue me ... to give me that easy way out. Even though I had grown the tiniest of backbones, I still had the strongest of aversions to confrontations ... especially with Mark.

On November 28, 2003 I was given a way out all right. Divine stepped in and indeed finally granted me my wish. However, it wasn't the easy way like I had prayed for. In fact, it was the most terrifying ordeal I'd ever have to endure.

The Night of Reckoning

———————— ∞ ————————

That morning I woke up, got all three children safely off to school, saw Mark off to work for the day, cleaned up the house throughout the afternoon, and then began supper preparations. Initially the day went like any other; that is until later that afternoon ...

All three children returned home from school right on schedule. Supper was soon to be ready, but Mark was running late. Where was Mark? He usually arrived home from work by four-thirty at the latest. After waiting an extra hour, I gave in to my children's hungry pleas and fed them. I put Mark's and my own supper plates in the oven to keep warm, and continuously stared at the clock in the kitchen. By nine o'clock that night there was still no sign of Mark. I bathed and put my children to bed, and resigned myself to the fact that Mark was likely at the bar drinking himself into yet another crazed stupor. In that moment, I felt the spirit of my grandmother surround me ... and I swore I could hear her voice in my mind:

"My darling Lisa you need to prepare yourself now. I know I used to say that a watched pot never boils, but tonight I have to eat my own words and tell you: WATCH THAT DAMN POT!"

Sheer panic and dread washed over me like it had never done before. I remember thinking to myself, "Okay. Something is very different right now, but I have absolutely no clue what the hell it is. I have to keep busy. Stop pacing the floor! Oh God help me what am I to expect tonight now? Maybe I should go downstairs and sit with Kevin. But I have to make sure I'm not down there when Mark gets here. Oh I'll hear the bike a mile away. I'll have plenty of time."

Kevin was one of Mark's younger cousins. He had been living with Mark and I for the last two years of our marriage, and he had become my number one confidant when it came to his cousin. He witnessed first-hand so many occasions where Mark had beaten or tormented me ... and by this time he had had enough of it.

"I swear to God Lisa," Kevin took my hand in his and stared intently into my eyes. "If he raises just one finger at you, I'll kill him. I kid you not."

"Please Kevin," my anxiety escalated ten-fold. "Don't say or do anything. You do anything then I'm just going to get it twice as bad and you know it. Please don't."

"No! I've had enough Lisa! He treats you like garbage all the time, and I am sick and tired of seeing it. If he does something tonight, I *will* get involved. I guarantee you. I'm not holding back anymore."

"OH NO! Here he comes!" I heard Mark in the not-too-far distance; shifting the bike up into first, second and then third gear as he made the turn down onto our road and started roaring towards the house. Normally the sound of the rumbling thunder would send me into a state of true bliss and awe. Not this time. Panicked, I bolt up the stairs leading to the living room as fast as my legs could carry me. Trying to take two stairs at a time, I missed the edge of one step and stumbled back down with a massive thud ... smashing my right knee on the edge. Not skipping a beat or even feeling the shooting pain in my knee (which I'll feel the next day), just like I had done all those years ago in that cheeseburger incident, I immediately picked myself up and scrambled the rest of the way up the stairs.

Just as I reached the couch and threw myself down onto it to make it look like I was watching tv, I heard the automatic garage door open and the bike rumble in. I heard the kickstand creak as Mark swung it down with his foot. He shut off the bike ... and there was then utter silence. I didn't even hear Mark walk around in his heavy biker boots. There was nothing. It's like he was contemplating whether or not he should get up off the bike. He was just sitting there! After an agonizing few seconds, I finally hear the all-too familiar sound of a helmet being hurled into concrete. The garage door closed and the door leading from the garage into the house opened. Oh hell ... here we go ...

———∿∿◦◦◠◠◠◦◦∿∿———

"Do you still want supper?" I asked nervously from my perch on the couch. "I put it in the oven to keep it warm." I then get up and hurriedly make my way out to the kitchen ... just in case he did want me to be the 'obedient servant' and fetch him his supper.

"Screw supper." Mark brushed past me, reached into the fridge, grabbed a beer, and sat down at the kitchen table. He cracked open the bottle of beer, took a huge swig, and set it down beside him on the table. He sat back, chest puffed out like a rooster about to blast out his alarm at the crack of dawn, and poised an out-turned hand on his thigh. Watching this particularly threatening body language told me that I definitely needed to brace myself. He was absolutely drop down, flat out, stinking hammered. Those demons within him were especially fiery this night – I could see their spirits dancing in his eyes ... just waiting to be unleashed. Mark cleared his throat:

"You know," he growled. "I am so bloody fed up. I work my ass off supporting you and these damn kids, yet I never have a thing to show for it." He turned and glared at me so intensely – if looks could kill I would have been dead right then and there. Yes ... this was going to be a bad one. One of the worst I'd see in a long while.

"Well what do you want me to do?" I pled.

"Oh f-k off!" Mark roared. "Look at Jim and Tammy next door! They have two kids, they both have jobs, and look at how well they're doing. Why can't we be like that?"

"Now how is *that* comparison even fair?" I cried out desperately. Indeed. Tammy was a registered nurse, and Jim was some sort of computer programmer ... or something like that. So of course they had money! "Mark, they both have steady jobs. In fact, they have actual *careers* ... of which I tried to establish for myself but *someone* stopped me from pursuing it! Remember? You've done that to me twice now. I should say three times because the first time was when you made me get rid of my horses. I gave everything up ... every time ... FOR YOU!"

Well that was the wrong thing to say, for immediately in response the demons sprung forth. Mark lunged out from his chair and grabbed me by the throat; squeezing to the point where I began to gasp for air. I couldn't even cry out for help. All I could do was think about Kevin downstairs. I supposed he hadn't heard what had transpired so far. But little did I know he was actually eavesdropping the entire time. He was waiting ... I suppose giving me a chance to fight back? Mark then released me from his death grip and threw me up against the kitchen counter. Growling (yes literally growling) he turned and sat himself back down at the table.

"Oh I'm just so fed up. Gimme my supper."

———∿∿⌒∽⌒⌒⌒∽∿∿———

For approximately the next hour, all was quiet as Mark thankfully passed out in the bed. I was so horribly shaken I couldn't relax even for a moment. That was the first time he ever went as far as choking me – which to me was a severe step up from a punch in the head. I was so fearful that Mark would wake up to once more continue with his rage. In an attempt to stop myself from wearing a rut in the floor, I decided that perhaps a nice hot bath would soothe my nerves. I snuck into the bedroom as quietly as I possibly could in order to retrieve my bathrobe and pajamas. Mark didn't stir even an inch. Thinking I was successful in that mini quest, I breathed a huge sigh of relief and started to run my bathwater.

The tub didn't even fill a quarter of the way when all of a sudden the bathroom door was violently kicked in. It swung open with such force that it knocked me off balance and sent me careening into the corner; I desperately clutched onto the back of the toilet for fear of smashing my face into it. Oh God the devil has awoken once more.

"Mark! I'm having a bath! Why did you do that for?"

"Having a bath," Mark sneered. "You're just in there trying to wash away the stench of sex aren't you?" Again? I couldn't believe he was once again accusing me of such a thing. I had to bite my tongue in an attempt to fight the urge to blurt out, "I'd love to know with whom you speak of."

"No!" I started to yell. I made sure to raise my voice so that Kevin could hear the commotion. At this point I started to strongly believe that I seriously *needed* Kevin to step in. "Of course not! I told you I'm just trying to have a bath to calm my nerves."

"F-ing bullshit!" Mark's demons roared into life. Trying to shield myself from Mark's deadly blows, I stood right behind the bathroom door. With the way that the bathroom was built, Mark couldn't quite reach me. It was a rather small bathroom, with the toilet situated directly behind the bathroom door whenever it was open. It was quite the commotion at this point: I was shoving back at Mark with the entire door, while Mark was thrusting the door in at me and swinging with his right fist around the corner. His wild fist swinging only managed to graze my left shoulder. It didn't even leave a bruise. That was some good shielding right there if you ask me. Doors make awesome barriers when you know how to use them.

"Mark! Stop it! Get out of here! Stop! Mark! Please ... stop!" I was frantically screaming in absolute terror. My terror was so great that I was beyond the point of shedding tears. I couldn't cry. All I did was yell and scream ... I believe today all in order for ANYONE and EVERYONE to hear my pleas. It worked ... Kevin bellowed at Mark from downstairs,

"What is going on? Leave her alone!"

"F-k off!" Mark yelled right back at him. "Mind your own business!"

"What you're doing *is* my business! Come here and do that to me you coward!"

I don't know what made Mark stop his wild madman door attack; perhaps it was Kevin having called him a coward. I still don't know the real reason, but whatever the reason, I was extremely grateful. Mark staggered back out to the kitchen and sat in his usual chair in the corner; leaving me sitting on the toilet, sobbing uncontrollably. Strangely, there were no actual tears ... just dry heaving sobs. While Mark and Kevin exchanged some unidentifiable insults, and I tried to regain some sense of composure, my dear eight year-old son snuck into his twin sisters' bedroom, gathered them up, took them into his room, and silently closed his door so that no one would notice or hear. Apparently that is where he kept them all night.

After I would have to say ten to fifteen minutes ... all was quiet once more. However, I was so petrified of leaving my safe haven in the bathroom it took me another five minutes just to gather my courage to take those first few steps out into the hall. With it so quiet, I had every hope that perhaps Mark had passed out once more. Stalling as long as I could, I drained the water out of the bathtub and neatly folded my robe and pajamas that got thrown to the floor in my struggles.

Realizing I could do no more to stall myself, carefully and quietly I tiptoed down the hall towards the living room. In doing so, I made the conscious effort to stay to my far left ... as I knew I had to pass the kitchen and the corner where Mark sat. Reaching the corner, I was utterly dismayed: there was Mark sitting there: wild wide eyes, tomato-red face (which was due to his high blood pressure), and of course a nice frosty beer in his hand. He didn't even look up at me as I walked past him. Good ... maybe he *is* done for the night, I thought.

I continued to make my way towards the couch, and spotted a full load of clean laundry in the hamper that I had forgotten to fold and put away. Insisting that I try to keep myself and my mind busy, I picked up the hamper. As if I was about to sit down onto a bunch of pins or needles, I carefully lowered myself onto the couch. I started to silently fold my laundry. Not a single word was spoken for a good five or ten minutes. Of course it was Mark who finally broke that silence.

"Witch!" Again Mark didn't actually use the word 'witch.' It was the infamously venomous four-letter 'c' word. "Witch. F-ING WITCH!" Without even the slightest of warnings Mark sprung from his chair and leapt across the living room – I swear the man grew wings because he reached me in a matter of two seconds, and I don't even think his feet hit the floor. It happened so fast I didn't quite know what hit me at first ... I just 'magically' found myself being pinned down on the couch and getting battered in the head punch after punch after punch.

I tried to shield Mark's flailing fists the best I could with my forearms, but a few still got past me. At one point I dodged left when I should have dodged right ... Mark caught me a good one ...and broke two of my teeth. That didn't stop him. If anything the sight of my broken teeth encouraged Mark's demonic rage even more. I continued to get pummelled; harder and harder he was swinging.

"No! Mark, get off of me! Get away from me! Stop it! No! Stop! Stop! Go away!" I screamed as loud as I could. Yet again there were no tears. I was way beyond tears. I remember actually trying to force myself to cry ... it wouldn't come. My Higher

Self just wouldn't allow it. Through my wielding forearms I peered up at Mark as he continued his battering rampage. I stared right into his eyes ... and while it was only for a split second, it felt like an eternity. What I saw within those eyes made my blood run cold. It wasn't Mark. Mark was no longer in residence. What I saw ... it was pure manic evil: totally void of any emotion other than extreme rage and hatred. I cannot describe that look accurately enough. No words can describe the coldness ... the death ... the evil intent. It was almost as if that man was truly demonically possessed. It's the closest I can come to in an accurate description, and even then it doesn't do it justice. But then again, how can one describe pure evil accurately?

The attack so far at this point had only lasted about a minute at most – but to me, even today, it felt like hours. And those eyes they will forever haunt me – no matter how much time passes.

I hear a loud thundering boom-boom-booming from the front foyer and stairs that led to the basement. Kevin!!!

Upon hearing the commotion of Kevin barrelling up the stairs, Mark immediately ceased his attack on me and turned his attention onto Kevin. I made the mistake of getting up off the couch: Kevin had a nine iron in his hands ...

Mark met Kevin at the top of the stairs and swung a drunken right hook to Kevin's head. As quick as a lightning bolt Kevin ducked out of the way, and in one sweeping motion swung the nine iron and connected with Mark squarely on his left rib cage.

KATHUD! Again Kevin swung the golf club and I hear a second sickening KATHUD! That mighty blow *had* to have broken a few ribs. It had to! Mark, even though he was clearly winded (as I heard him gasp for air as Kevin hit him), didn't stop. It's like he didn't even really feel the impact or pain – his adrenaline was obviously running in overdrive. He lunged right on top of Kevin – thus sending both of them careening over the edge of the stairs and rolling all the way down to the first landing ... the front foyer.

Having the great luck of landing on top of Mark, Kevin took the opportunity to pin him to the floor and started to whack his head off of the steel door that led out to the garage. BANG! BANG! BANG! As I watched all of this happening, I was now finally crying ... and screaming and pleading with them to stop. It was the most horrifying scene I've ever witnessed: especially two close family members duking it out in such extreme rage.

Kevin lost control or his footing or something, but that allowed Mark to get up off the floor. Kevin, now fearing for his own safety a little bit, tried to escape by leaping down the next flight of stairs into his bedroom. In doing so, all I heard was a loud and rather disturbing "katuck" sound ... that was Kevin's head smashing into the metal reinforced support beam over the stairway. He had one heck of a hard head because he actually dented that support beam!

Kevin landed on the cement floor of his basement bedroom. He saw stars swirling about his head and was dazed slightly, but he shook it off right away as he knew Mark was in hot pursuit.

I'm standing at the top of the stairs, Mark in the front foyer landing, and Kevin in the basement. I then see Mark eying something very precious to me: my late grandmother's antique marble table. That table was older than me – I have pictures of when I was two years old with that table sitting in the background. That table was also extra special to me because when my grandmother first had her stroke, that table was the absolute last thing of hers that she had touched – for the paramedics found the table overturned next to her body.

"No!!!!!" I bellowed out at Mark. I knew what he was thinking. "No! Don't you dare! No! Mark! Nooooooooo...." Mark picked up my Nana's marble table, heaved it above his head, and hurled it down into the basement at Kevin as hard as he possibly could. Upon impact with the cement floor, due to its fragile nature and age, it shattered into a million pieces ... quite literally. And me ... I shattered right along with it. I could take no more. I collapsed onto the floor ... wailing in deep despair, grief, and misery.

"No no no no ... no no ... Not my Nana's table. My poor Nana. The table. Oh god ... the table ... nooooooooooo no no no."

———

Still wailing on the floor and starting to feel a major asthma attack come on, I suddenly found myself being picked up by Mark. The energy ... it shifted completely. There was no more evil. No more intent to kill. Mark was back again ... loving, gentle, caring ... and deeply concerned.

"What's going on here?" Mark tenderly whispered as he carefully and lovingly picked me up off the floor. "What's going on? Come over here and sit down. You want some iced tea? I bought you some iced tea yesterday. Here ... sit down and I'll get you a glass." Mark slowly and gently guided me over to the kitchen table ... he even sat me down in his chair. I was never allowed to sit in his chair ... but here I was. Once he realized I was all right sitting there on my own, he walked over to the fridge, grabbed the pitcher of iced tea, poured me a glass and handed it to me like I was going to drop it or something. He was so thoughtful, caring and careful. Then, to make this even more disturbing and confusing, he stood right beside me and wouldn't leave my side. He stood there and gently rubbed my back in an effort to calm me down. I just sat there ... sipped my tea ... got my breathing and sobbing under control ... and didn't say a word. Kevin on the other hand heard every single word that Mark was saying to me. He called out from the basement,

"You know full well what's going on here you psychotic freak."

"You shut up," Mark growled at him. "You're out of here. I've had enough of you. You're out that door. I don't care where you go. This was the last straw you ingrate." Mark then turns to me and whispers, "That's it. I'm getting him out of here. We don't need his crap. I'm calling the cops."

It then dawned on me what was happening: Mark had completely blacked out everything that he had done to me earlier that night and has in turn transferred his anger and rage onto Kevin!

"Yeah, go ahead. Call the cops," Kevin countered. "I'll tell them the honest truth of what's going on here."

"Shut up!" Mark waited no longer. He snatched the phone up from the table and dialed 9-1-1, while I took the opportunity to get the hell out of the room. I holed myself up in the bathroom.

Of course I couldn't hear what the operator was saying to Mark, but Mark was trying to tell the operator that Kevin beat on him and that he wants him removed from the premises. Kevin however was right there to holler his statements out so that the operator could hear:

"Tell them the reason why I beat on you! Tell them what you were doing! Tell them you freak! Tell them that you were beating on your wife!"

The operator definitely heard Kevin yelling in the background because the next thing I knew Mark was beckoning for me to come out; the operator wanted to speak with me. As I took the phone from Mark, he gave me a loving wink and smile. Really?

"Hello miss," the operator says. "Can you please go into another room so that we can talk a little more openly?" I quickly complied with her request and hurriedly rushed into my bedroom and closed the door.

"Now," the operator continued. "I just want you to answer yes or no. Has your husband been hitting you this evening?"

"Yes." Oh boy with that answer I knew full well that there was no turning back now.

"Okay. I have already dispatched two officers to your location. But as a precaution I want you to remain on the line with me and stay in your room until they arrive. Do you understand?"

"Yes, I understand."

Within five minutes I heard the knock on the front door. The police had arrived. I informed the operator and hung up the phone. I sat there on the edge of my bed ... I waited and listened as they began to talk to Mark. Again Mark was trying to let on to the officers that he made the call against his cousin ... that Kevin had beaten him. Mark even showed the officers the welts that were already forming from where Kevin had hit him with the golf club. Kevin on the other hand wouldn't let up. He wanted the truth told. The officers called out to me – letting me know that it was safe for me to emerge from hiding. I slowly walk down the hall to meet the officers.

"Ma'am, is it true that your husband was hitting you tonight?" Mark looked at me expectantly. I swear he thought that I was totally going to back him up on his story. But you know, I couldn't even get a word out. Instead of speaking ... I burst out into a fresh bout of tears. That was all the police needed.

"Sir, if you didn't hit your wife then why did she just react that way?" Mark had no answer.

So Mark sealed his own fate by calling the police. It wasn't Kevin that the police escorted in handcuffs out of the home. It was Mark ...

Ironically (or not so ... I haven't quite figured which out yet), over the course of the entire fourteen years that I was with Mark, that was the first and only time the police were ever called in to investigate any domestic dispute between us.

The Journey Part One: In Limbo

Within seconds of Mark's arrest, I felt instantaneous relief. Yet at the same time I also felt extremely exhausted, lost, alone ... and terrified of what was to come next. I also had the very distinct but silent knowing that my prayers for a 'way out' had finally been answered ... and that no matter what I had to follow through on it. When Divine answered a prayer you don't back out on it. You just don't. I believe that creates even further bad karma. So, even though I was grateful for my answered prayers, at the same time I felt like my back was up against a wall. It petrified me to know that from that point on the world as I had always known it had ended – and I was clueless on how to move forward.

Mark was held in jail for approximately one week – as no one could go to post bail right away. He did in fact call me to demand that I bail him out, but I outright refused. Of course that angered Mark all over again, and like the perpetual never-ending cycle that it was, that in turn caused my fear to deepen all the more. Yeah right. I'm going to go right away and bail out a man that is threatening me? Not a chance! He can stay there! And stay there he did ... after a week he finally managed to get his work supervisor and a friend to post bail for him and sign as his surety.

Upon release on bail, Mark was banned from even going near the house let alone enter it. Furthermore, because his work supervisor signed as a surety, Mark had to live with him until the court date; which didn't occur until four months later. However, Mark never did listen to too many rules; there were three or four different days when he showed up completely unannounced – he just walked right in the door, and even slept there once. Could I not have removed him? Certainly I could have. But when you're scared out of your wits of someone who had beaten on you for so long, you tend to only worry about what would happen to you between the time that you call the police and the time they arrive to take him away. He could have killed me three times over in that period of time. He certainly had it in him to do it – I saw it in his eyes so strongly that night. So I never dared. I do wonder though why he did stop coming around. I often think that perhaps his friends advised him against it. I don't know ... I'm merely speculating at this point. Mark made it oh so clear to me though that he most certainly didn't agree with the rule at all. In fact, he was so resentful towards it he made darn sure that I suffered as a result.

"I own that house! I have every right to be in that house," Mark bellowed at me over the phone one evening.

"Yeah well you lose your rights when you get arrested for domestic violence," I barked back. "They do that to protect me and to protect the kids. And by the way I own this house too."

"Protect you?" Mark chuckled. "Protect you from what?"

"From you!" Right from that infamous 'Night of Reckoning' I knew that something wasn't 'right' with Mark's mind. The way that he switched from psychotic manic to soft and loving protector will forever haunt me. He seriously didn't remember what *really* happened – and right up to his death he *still* outright denied the actual events.

"Look I said it before and I'll say it again. *I didn't touch you!* There isn't even a mark on you!" I didn't even bother to argue with him. There was no point. That was something else I had learned all those years with him: he only heard what he wanted to hear and believed what he wanted to believe ... and no one was going to tell him otherwise truth or not.

"Whatever," I muttered weakly. Already my energy had been sucked dry by the conversation. Yet, I could tell by how Mark cleared his throat that he wasn't near done with me.

"Well, seeing as I'm not allowed to be in my own home, then I refuse to pay the bills for it!" And so therein lies Mark's warped way of thinking.

"What?!" At that point I literally couldn't believe what I was hearing. "Mark, you know full well that I don't work. How in the hell do you expect the bills to get paid then?"

"Humph!" Mark gave another chuckle. It was as if he thoroughly enjoyed causing such chaos. "That's not my problem. I'm not allowed there anymore."

"Mark," I began to reason with him. "I don't have any money. The mortgage is over two grand a month! Then there's the heat, electricity, phone, and cable. Need I mention food? What about the kids?"

"Not my problem," Mark stated matter-of-factly. "I don't live there anymore."

Mark then abruptly hung up the phone, and left me sitting at the kitchen table in panicked tears.

———⁓⁓⁓———

Three months pass, and no bills were paid. I had no job and of course had no savings to fall back on; Mark made sure of that a year prior when he drained my entire inheritance account. As a result, our mortgage went into default: the bank grew just a tad angry and decided to pursue legal foreclosure action against us. The cable got disconnected, and the natural gas for our heating was *going* to be disconnected – that was until they learned that I had three young children in the home (and at that time we were still in the midst of winter). The same went with the electricity; they were going to disconnect service until they realized that I had children. So at least I was bought some time with the heat and electricity – I had exactly two months to figure something out.

Mark left me hanging high and dry and in true dire straits. Not knowing what else to do, I tried applying for emergency social assistance. Even after telling the case worker the entire truth of the story and how desperate I was just to get food in the house for my children, they wouldn't help me. Why? Because at that time, when they did the initial intakes for assistance, they took all government credit payments into account when trying to establish household income ... including the monthly Mother's Allowance (which is now called the Canada Child Tax Credit Benefit). Whatever income is made by any person in the home, it is automatically subtracted from the amount that social assistance would give. Well, based on their calculations, my monthly benefit amount pretty much wiped out the money that they would give me! It would have left me with a whopping thirty dollars. So there was no point.

At a loss, I confided in one of the neighbours by telling her all that happened and what I was up against. Immediately she packed me up in her car and drove me to her church to give me three massive boxes full of whatever food she could possibly find. She was a true blessing and angel – for she got my children and I through those first few months with the support of her church.

———∿∿∾⊙⊱⊙⊰⊙∿∾∿———

Another three months pass, and still I am struggling. Mark's cousin stayed with me to help with the kids, but he didn't have a job so couldn't help pay the bills or buy groceries. However, I finally made at least a little bit of progress by that time: I found a new job with another online psychic website. It didn't pay much, but at least it was something. At least I could pay the electricity and bring some food into the house! I should say that grocery shopping was a *major mission* for me: because Mark's truck bit the biscuit (the steering column blew on it), he took it upon himself to claim my beloved Camaro (of which I bought for myself for a mere hundred dollars – absolutely nothing was wrong with it ... well ... other than the fact that to this day I believe it was possessed). He made the excuse that he needed to get to and from work – and with snow still on the ground he clearly couldn't ride the Harley. I couldn't stop him. Not even legally. Why you ask? Because ... and this is where my stupidity once again ran rampant: for insurance purposes only I put my Camaro into Mark's name! Needless to say I never drove my car again ... and he ran it into its grave only a few months after him getting his hands on it.

Anyways back to what I was saying here: getting groceries was a major mission. I had to walk. Realize we did not live in a city or even a town. We lived in what I'll call the "semi-country": just far enough away from everything that it takes eons to get there. The grocery store, while only a fifteen minute drive, was a two and a half hour walk! I know ... I walked it. I tried to make a nice trip out of it though: leaving my three children in the care of their older half-brother, I'd walk alongside the railroad tracks that were no longer in use so that I could journey through the bushes and wee forest. I'd have to stop a few times to take a breather, so my usual "break point" was a beautiful fast-running stream that ran through a patch of heavy shade. It was perfect! I remember I almost fell asleep a few times listening to the chirping birds and long reeds blowing in the gentle breeze. I remember just dreading the walk (for by the time I reached the grocery store I was dead on my feet), but yet also looking forward to it. It was then when I could think more clearly ... and listen to my inner guidance and wisdom ... and indeed receive some divine messages of my own. The only questions I wanted answered were: What do I do? What is to happen next? Will life always be this difficult – and if not when will it get better? Where do I go? How do I move forward? Who is going to be there for me? Will I always be alone?

It was during one of my grocery walks that I received some of the most profound divine guidance *ever.*

* Oh by the way, no I never walked back with the groceries. Are you crazy? I managed to keep just enough for a taxi ride home. Hey, come on you guys! I'm not a pack mule you know.

———∿∿○○ᘓᕔᘒᕤᘓᕔ○∿∿———

March of 2004, Mark and I put our home up for sale before the bank could finalize the foreclosure proceedings. It sold very quickly: in a matter of three weeks at the most! We worked together in dealing with the real estate agents – when we had to (most other times Mark would request that they meet him in his regular bar for any sort of contract signings). By this time I was in a real state of panic – I was refusing to return to Mark, but I also still had absolutely no idea where I was going or what I was doing. I was still that lonely, lost puppy. One of my high school friends had me almost talked into going into subsidized housing where she was, but something about it all disturbed me. I just didn't like the idea for some reason. I felt like I was whacking my head into a brick wall; I just wasn't getting anywhere. Until I had to go on my "grocery walk" on day ...

"I don't want to go back to renting a place," I said to myself. "I most certainly don't want to go live by Kate in that damn subsidized housing either! Going through with either of those ideas would just make me go backwards in progress. I was a homeowner here so I am going to continue being a homeowner. But how? How can I do this? Even renting around here the cost of living will kill me. I just won't be able to survive. What to do?" Then that all-too familiar voice of my spirit guide at the time whispered in my mind:

"If you want to remain a homeowner, you must move north. If you want to survive as you say, then move north. You're right. You will not make it if you stay down here – not anywhere here in southern Ontario. SO MOVE NORTH!"

Move north. I immediately agreed – that was an awesome idea. To make me even more excited about it, I then had the additional thought that the further away I got from Mark the better. And ... I wouldn't tell him a damn thing either!

Once I returned home with the groceries I set straight to work on the computer; searching up properties for sale in northern Ontario. What helped was I knew approximately how much I would be receiving from the sale of our home, so at least I had a general budget to work with. My search didn't last long – I believe it lasted for a matter of just two hours. A property caught my eye – the price was right ... and there was something about the energy of the place that drew me in. I just couldn't ignore the strong magnetic attraction ... I believe I even thought to myself "this is my castle." Even certain numbers in the listing spoke to me; like the street address and dimensions of the different rooms. I just listened to my gut instinct. I couldn't help it. I called my real estate agents first thing the following morning to try and set up a time for me to view the home. But how would I get there? I had no vehicle! What was I going to do? Walk the entire way there and back? I didn't know ... nor did I care. I just knew that I had to make the trip to Iroquois Falls to see that house. I just placed my trust in Divine and the Universe and thought, "If it is meant to be then something will come through. I'm just following my gut here."

———⟨∿∘ତ⃝ତ⃝∘∿⟩———

Three days later and at five o'clock in the morning I found myself packing my three children into the back seat of a used grey Ford car that Mark signed over to me (which I know full well one of his friends *made* him do!). And of course Kevin accompanied us on the trip; as it was an eight hour non-stop drive ... I couldn't have driven a full sixteen hours all by myself.

Arriving in Iroquois Falls at around one in the afternoon, the five of us marvelled at how beautiful and quaint the town truly was. I was also struck immediately with the very friendly and loving energy that was flowing throughout the entire area. As we slowly drove through the tiny town of less than four thousand, all I could think was wow ... what a gorgeous place to raise my children! Nestled snugly amongst the many lakes, rivers, and forests for as far as the eyes can see, Iroquois Falls immediately felt like home to me. Yet, I had never heard of Iroquois Falls in my life let alone even been in the area before.

Having worked our way through to the furthest part of the town, we finally pulled into the driveway of the house I wanted to look at. I tiredly put the car into park and slowly got out of the car – not once taking my eyes off of the house. There it was: a 1250 square-foot, two-storey, three bedroom home. Yes, it did need a bit of work: the yellow stucco was peeling and the brown roof shingles were falling apart. Well come on give the house a break ... after all it was 90 years old. But I think my mind was made up before I even got out of the car. The house was mine.

As I took the key out of the real estate's lock box and unlocked the door, I once again heard the voice of my spirit guide:

"Welcome home, Lisa. It's taken you many years to return, but here you are. Be happy and know that you are loved. This is just the beginning."

The five of us stayed at the house for about an hour – the children were even excitedly picking out their rooms already! Well, I thought to myself, if that wasn't a sign then I didn't know what was. After a brief rest, we packed ourselves up in the car and made the long eight hour journey back south. And I was full of resolve ... and the amount of personal power that I felt was almost overwhelming – for realize I never felt empowered in my life ... not until those moments.

———⁓ʍⱺⱺⱺⱺ⁓———

"Yes this is Lisa." The following morning, right at the crack of eight, I called up my real estate agents. "I drove up to view that house yesterday. I want to put an offer on it please."

"Are you serious?" The lady agent questioned. "Oh my god how did you drive all that way and make it back? You did it all in one shot?"

"It wasn't easy, but yes I did."

"Wow! Well okay. What were they asking now for that place?"

"The listing has the asking price at $19,900."

"That's right too. That's a foreclosure sale. I spoke to the agent up there about that. Weird how you found this place and your home was in the process of foreclosure too before it closed. Talk about ironic or what? Okay let's get down to business here. What is your offer and your proposed closing date?"

"I want to put an offer in of $14,500, and I want the closing date to be the exact same closing date as our house here. So the fourth of June," I seriously do not know why I chose that particular amount. I mean why I even wanted to talk them down was beyond me because even paying the full price of what they were asking I still would have had some money left over to buy furniture, food and so forth. But that's what I did ... I just went with it. The worst they could say was 'no' and make a counter offer.

"Okay," the real estate agent clearly sounded skeptical. "I'll put the offer in right away. But just so you know, because this is a foreclosure sale, they usually don't accept offers too far off from the full asking price. Your offer is way down there. So be prepared for a denial, Lisa."

"That's fine. I'm prepared for that. We'll see what happens," I then nervously added: "And by the way, please do not mention any of this to Mark. I do not want him knowing where I'm going or what I'm doing. Not until I have completely moved there."

"Don't worry sweetheart," the agent reassured. She knew everything that happened as one of the first questions you're asked when listing a home for sale is why you are selling to begin with. I certainly didn't hold anything back ... and Mark's behavior with her and her husband in their dealings with him over the sale just solidified and confirmed it all for them. I remember how appalled they were when he requested that they meet him in a bar, of all places, to sign the closing documents. "Neither one of us will say a word. We'll do what we can for you. I promise."

I hung up the phone and started my usual pacing of the floor. I prayed with all my might that my offer would be accepted. I needed a direction to travel in … and the purchase of that home would give that to me. If it's one thing that I absolutely hate even to this day is that of being kept in a state of confused limbo!

———∿∿·⊙⊙⊙✦⊙⊙∿∿———

Later that same night the phone rang. It was Mark. Of course. Just what I needed! Whoo hoo!

"We need to talk," Mark began. Oh great, I thought. Here we go again. He's going to try and talk me into going back with him. Not a chance in hell. Forget it. Especially after what he had done to me and the children the past few months since he got arrested. He had definitely shown some of his true colors to me over those months. Never again!

"What about now?"

"Well," Mark cleared his throat, and I could hear the distinct rumblings of those demons in his voice. He was looking for a fight this time. "I've decided that when the sale of the house closes, I want you to give me the money that you owe me."

"What?!" I was totally shocked. "What money? I don't owe you a damn thing! If anything, you owe me money for child support these past few months. You haven't done anything for the kids at all."

"Oh yes," Mark hissed. "You owe me. I supported you all these years you're damn right you're going to pay me back now. I want my credit cards paid off. I want the loan paid off. And the gas and hydro and cable bills paid off. And I'm not paying you a cent in child support." Oh you can bet I was fuming at this point.

"What about the addition on the house that I paid for," I countered. "And the Harley? And my having paid off both your credit cards two years ago? By rights if you want to keep that bike then you need to give me *at least* half of what I paid for it! You also drove my Camaro into the grave so you owe me for that too."

"Ha ha!" Mark was actually laughing! "You're not getting any money for the bike! And yeah you're damn right you paid. Like I said. I supported you all of these years. It's time to pay up. And child support? Yeah right. You're the one that wanted to leave. Remember? I'm not paying. You make me do that; I'll just up and quit work. Simple."

I couldn't get another word in edge-wise as at that Mark abruptly hung up the phone. I was extremely irate, perplexed, and utterly speechless. And I knew too that there was nothing that I could legally do. I couldn't prove that the Camaro was actually mine, nor could I prove that the Harley was really mine ... both were in Mark's name for insurance purposes! All I had as "proof" that I paid for the Harley was a copy of the generalized bank draft made out to our friend's widow for the amount of $18,000. Nor could I take Mark to court to get a child support order: I couldn't afford a lawyer and I refused to go to legal aid because back in those days if you used their services, they would put a lien on your home (social services did that too by the way). I felt trapped ... and at a total loss.

An anxiety-riddled twenty-four hours passed when finally the long-awaited call came in from the real estate agent. She had an answer to my offer. With trembling hands I pick up the phone and nervously listen to the voice on the other end.

"Lisa!" the agent was quite excited. "I don't know how you did this. In all my twenty years of working in real estate I have *never* seen this before. Lisa, they accepted your offer. Did you know, $14,500 was actually the absolute lowest offer that they were going to accept? I don't know how you did it or how you even thought to come up with that specific offer amount, but Lisa congratulations. You're moving to Iroquois Falls."

Words cannot express how happy, excited ... and surprised I was in that moment. I swear if I hadn't have been sitting down I would have fallen down from the explosion of energy and emotion. I got my direction. Now it was just a case of me needing to put one foot in front of the other and follow it.

———— ✦✦✦✦✦✦ ————

"I dare you to show up in that courtroom. Go ahead! Go ahead and testify against me! See what happens. I dare you." Mark sneered over the phone. He was panicking as the all-mighty court date was a mere two days away. He also came to realize, somehow, that perhaps he had in fact done something 'wrong.' The Crown Attorney's Office (or District Attorney as it would be in the United States), was looking for serious jail time for Mark. And he was trying to do all that he could to stop that from happening.

"I'm going," I stood firm. I wasn't going to let Mark get to me any longer. He pushed me too far beyond by that point. "No, I don't like the idea of you having to go to jail. But I have no choice. I have to go. I may not have laid any charges but *they – the cops* did. As a result I am being forced to go. The cops are picking me up here in the morning to take me to court."

"Just see what happens if you go," that was the only statement Mark could muster at that point. I believe he was getting more flustered by my sheer refusal to submit and obey like I always had done before.

"Yes, I shall." Then it was my turn to hang up the phone on *him*.

———∿∿∾∾⧫⧫∾∾∿∿———

Court day – 10am. I found myself sitting in the Crown Attorney's office under their protection. The attorney informed me that Mark's defense lawyer had the desire to possibly enter in a plea bargain: if Mark were to plead guilty, instead of sending him to jail he would be put on probation and sent to counseling. The reason for this was their concern that he wouldn't be able to provide for the children if put in jail. I tried to argue by informing the attorney that Mark hadn't done a darn thing for them yet – so what would the difference really be? But then Mark's words from our last conversation echoed in my head. Well, I thought, I will be the bigger person here and will agree to it. Perhaps *then* I may get somewhere with that man in terms of support.

The Crown Attorney made me stay in his office throughout the entire duration of the court proceeding, and wouldn't even let me leave until he knew that Mark had left the courthouse parking lot. The plea bargain was accepted by the judge. Mark therefore received eighteen months' probation (with the strict stipulation that he was not to communicate with or be around me in any way for the duration of his probation period) and ordered to attend anger management counseling as well as a course for domestic violence awareness.

For the record: Mark never did go to any course for domestic violence awareness, and he only attended *one meeting* with a therapist for anger management. You want to know why? I'll tell you: Mark put on such a great show for the therapist, the therapist ruled that he did not need counseling! To this day I cannot figure that one out. How a therapist could overrule a judge's court order is beyond me. But okay ... apparently Mark didn't have anger management issues? And indeed – for years afterwards he would still pull that particular card out of his hat to play against me: whenever the topic of his arrest and charge was brought up, he denied ever touching me ... and would repeat the words of that therapist that he didn't need any counseling.

—⁓⦿⦿⦿⦿⦿⁓—

June 4, 2004 – moving day! I don't know why, but I severely procrastinated in packing for the move. Perhaps, on a more subconscious level, it was my fear that was paralyzing me: fear of the unknown, fear of failure, fear of not being able to make it financially, fear of being alone. All of those fears came creeping back in to haunt me during those last few days and hours in our old home. But there was no turning back then. Our house had sold, and I bought my own home … eight hours away. And yes … that realization of all that in itself freaked me out even more. Yet I had no choice. I had my three beautiful children to take care of. And I would prove from there on in that I would do *anything* to make sure that they were safe, loved, and well looked after. Even if that meant me having to turn away from all the money that I did factually lose to Mark: the Camaro, the Harley, the addition, the credit cards. None of that mattered anymore. All I could think about was getting the hell out of there and as far away from him as possible. I needed to take care of those kids. They were top priority. And no, I never did receive any compensation for a single thing. Right up until his passing, Mark had kept "my" Harley that I paid for all those years ago. Am I resentful? Yes. Just a tad … but I did what I had to do in those moments.

At any rate, you can also count on Mark having stopped in to try and ask questions on moving day. Thankfully my brother was there helping Kevin and I load the massive twenty-four foot moving truck that I had rented. He was able to keep Mark away from me; and *he* filled Mark in on what was happening. But because of my procrastination in packing, we didn't get out of there until close to six in the evening ... which resulted in us arriving in Iroquois Falls in the wee hours of the morning. It was good in a way though, as all three children slept pretty much the entire way. But oh boy was it darn cold when we arrived! I remember fumbling around in the darkness trying to get the key for the door out of the lock box as fast as I could. To us it felt like we were suddenly teleported back six months to the dead of winter. I'm telling you it was so chilly, I could see my breath.

Finally inside, the five of us made make-shift beds on the softly carpeted living room floor and quickly fell into I believe one of the soundest sleeps any of us had in years. But before doing so, I distinctly remember sleepily gazing up at the ceiling.

"We're home," I state out loud for the kids and Kevin to hear. "Oh .... Oh wow how pretty. Look at that. My ceiling is all sparkly like it has pink, purple and blue fairy dust in it."

I think I was overtired by that point. Ha ha!

The Journey Part Two: Survival of the Fittest & Pursuing Dreams

With Iroquois Falls being quite the close-knit small community, I knew that we would have been the talk of the town for the first few days: "A southern single mother just bought that vacant house. Wonder what brought her all the way up here? I bet she has a lot of work to do – that house has been sitting empty for the last four years." Well, over the course of the first six months to year I was proven right ... but definitely in a good way.

I was in a totally alien world. I was completely alone ... well of course I had my three children, and Kevin likewise stayed with us for quite a while (as he had no place to go as a result of what he had done to his cousin with that golf club – most of their family somewhat shunned him afterwards – although in their defense none of them knew how Mark really was). But I had no one else. I didn't know a single soul in the entire area, and even my brother, alongside his father (my stepfather), decided to turn his back on me. The two of them came to the conclusion that I was horrible for moving so far away. Ultimately they didn't support my decisions. But the love and support of my new community got me through ... as you will see as we move forward. Even the kids' new school principal came to my home to introduce himself to me and took us on a tour of the school itself. I felt very warmly welcomed by all who approached me.

The very first day here my new neighbours walked over to introduce themselves, and they even helped us to unload the truck. This encouraged me greatly; for the first time I felt like I received confirmation from *outside* of my own guidance that I made the right move.

For the first time in my entire life I finally felt in control. I had freedom that I never had before and a sense of true empowerment. I also came to the realization that I likewise had something that not too many folks could say: I had my own castle – which I owned outright: no mortgage at all and most certainly no rent. I was finally excited about my brand new life. And nothing was going to stop me.

———ᴡᴡᴏᴏᴏᴏᴏᴏᴏᴡᴡ———

July 1, 2004 – Canada Day, the town held a wonderful celebration at the park just up the road from my house. Kevin had taken the three children for a walk to investigate the goings-on. They were gone not even ten minutes when one of my six year old girls came bursting through the door.

"Mommy! Mommy you have to come," she gasped for air. She obviously ran all the way down to the house. I looked up from the reading that I was preparing on my computer, wondering what she could possibly be so excited about.

"Why? What's wrong? You know Mommy is trying to get this work done. I'll go later."

"No!" What? Did my child just say 'no' to me? Ha ha! "Mommy *please* come now. Mommy they have horses up there! You gotta come see! People are riding them."

Well that little girl definitely knew her mother. She knew that I had a deep passion for horses, and she also knew that I had always worked with horses up until the time I moved to Vancouver with Mark. She didn't need to say another word. I completely forgot about the backlog of readings I needed to get done, and taking her tiny hand in mine we walked together back up to the park.

Even through the crowd of fellow townsfolk and thick line of bushes I immediately spotted the horses. There were only two of them: a handsome palomino quarter horse and a stunning chocolate-colored mustang mare. A young blonde girl and a tall, muscular gentleman wearing a brown cowboy hat were leading the horses around; giving people a brief ride. The line-up for the horse ride was pretty darn long ... but I didn't care! I was getting on one of them if it killed me. After waiting for what felt like eons, finally we reached the point where we were next in line. I started to walk up towards the cowboy man. All of a sudden I felt nervous. Why did I feel so nervous? For pete sake I have been riding since I was three years old. I've taken out trail rides in the mountains and jumped Olympic-sized jumps. Riding a horse is like riding a bike – you may be rusty at first but you don't ever fully forget how. I didn't understand why I was so nervous so suddenly, but I had to do something to get rid of it ... or hide it. I hastily tried to think of something to say to cowboy man. I turned to him and smiled.

"Your horses are absolutely gorgeous," I couldn't think of anything else to say! Quick Lisa. For god sake you look like a fool! "They are so calm and good-natured too around all these people." There you go. At least it was something. Dumbass!

"Well thank you. Thank you very much," cowboy man nodded his acknowledgment and smiled. Wow he had quite the thick French accent ... which just simply reminded me of where I actually was. However I couldn't help but think to myself how cool it was: a French cowboy! It was obvious that he was rushing around and didn't have time for idle chitchat. I didn't blame him ... I'm sure he wanted to get through the rides as smoothly and quickly as possible. After all it was a sweltering hot day and the horses would need to be watered and fed. He then turned to my one daughter,

"Which horse would you like to ride?" he pointed over to the gelding first. "There's Mr Chevy over there, and there's Running Running Chinook right here."

"I don't wanna run," my daughter replied. Laughing at my daughter's purely innocent remark, cowboy man nodded once more and gently lifted her up onto Mr Chevy's back. Taking it that this was my cue, I informed that I would get on Chevy with her while Kevin accompanied my other daughter on Chinook. My son already had a ride much earlier, so he just stood there to watch. I was hoping that cowboy man was going to lead us around instead of his teenage helper so that I could try to strike up more conversation with him, but unfortunately that didn't happen. It seemed to me that it was of great importance that he was the one to lead Chinook around. Oh well. It just would have been nice to talk to someone – to get to know at least one person in my new town.

After we had our round-a-bout ride, cowboy man met us once again to help my daughter down. I dismounted myself, gave him a smile, and thanked him for allowing us to have a ride on his awesome horses.

"Oh you're very welcome my dear. It was my pleasure," cowboy man smiled and gestured over to Chinook and Chevy. "And theirs too!"

Having accomplished my main mission, I gathered my children and headed back home. From that point on I had a new mission: now that Mark was out of my life and couldn't control a damn thing that I did, I was bound and determined that *someday* I would have my horses again. And who was that cowboy man by the way? For some strange reason he too seemed to linger in the back of my mind for a day or two afterwards. His energy made me feel like he was quite the unique and interesting individual. Too bad I didn't get a chance to talk to him or get to know him more.

My first winter and Christmas here was total chaos. Firstly, my furnace decided to just up and die on me (which is not a good thing up in these parts – winter temperatures quite frequently plummet to -35C to -40C). Thankfully, another loving neighbour came to fix my furnace for me for free. However that didn't squash the turmoil I was going through. In fact, my furnace dying just compounded my negative thought process – it made me realize just how alone and vulnerable I really was. I was going through quite the emotional rollercoaster, and I also have to admit that I was likewise experiencing severe financial difficulties.

Realize that it was my very first Christmas away from Mark ... and away from all that I had ever known. In years prior, I always would go out of my way to ensure that *everyone* had a great Christmas: I'd bake up a storm, cook a huge turkey dinner, and pile so many presents under the tree that one year I think I actually managed to have more gifts than tree in my living room! Not this year. This year I was truly struggling to survive. Sure, I didn't have a mortgage or rent to worry about. But I still had all the other utility bills to pay, buy groceries, and winter clothing for the kids. As I had mentioned earlier, I couldn't receive social assistance (even if I financially qualified I'd *still* have to actually sell my home first!), and I was lucky to make $400 a month with that online psychic website. I only had that and the monthly government benefit that I always received for the children to rely on. It wasn't much. Once all the bills were paid, I was literally left with nothing. And actually, because I felt so pressured for Christmas, I fell *behind* in all the utility bills by a month. I didn't want my kids to go without, so I reneged on the utility bills for November. As a result of that, I was always in debt – even after paying them each month. And that indebtedness lasted for another year to year and a half! I'm going to come clean with you right now: there were days when it was so bad that I couldn't even afford a loaf of bread or bag of milk. As a result I would actually go without eating just to ensure that my children had something to eat. I would also approach my boss at the psychic website and inform her of what was going on. So she would try to send me an advance on my pay – even if it was $40 – just to get me through. Unfortunately, I even had to go as far as hocking off my old wedding ring from Mark and my late grandmother's Royal Doulton dolls. I did whatever I possibly could just to get by.

I remember having the most serious nervous breakdown one night just before Christmas. I put all three children to bed, sat on the couch, and turned the tv on. That was my mistake right there: showing that night was the movie "A Christmas Story," and I just happened to turn it on where the family was gathered around opening up all their gifts. I saw that and just emotionally shattered to pieces. I began to wail like a little baby. Poor Kevin ... he didn't know what to say or do other than put an arm around me and silently hold me until I stopped.

I will never forget that first Christmas – not just because of my emotional breakdown – but also because of the outpouring of love and support that came from the community of Iroquois Falls. It's hard not to shed a few tears as I relate to you this part of my journey ...

Somehow the community knew everything that I had gone through: my abusive marriage and recent separation from Mark, my financial struggling, my emotional state. I didn't talk to anyone, so I seriously do not know – not even to this day – how they knew. But they did ... and they did what they could to support me.

Because Iroquois Falls doesn't have a mall or many stores to buy Christmas gifts in (and the car that Mark had signed over to me crapped out), one neighbour drove me to a neighbouring town so that I could get at least a few things for the kids. I couldn't get much, but I got what I could.

Another loving neighbour knocked on my back door one day. There she was standing there in -25C temperatures with two *massive* cardboard boxes. The boxes were so large you could fit a 32-inch television in each of them. Both of the boxes were literally stuffed to the brims with canned goods, a lot of homemade baked goodies like tarts, cookies, and traditional French tortieres (meat pies), a turkey, bread, milk, and oh God I can't even remember all of the food that was in those boxes!

Then for another super surprise (and a very emotional one): two days before Christmas I just happen to look out the back door and see a Santa start to walk up towards my house. Well, it was more like he was staggering as if drunk – because I didn't even have a snow shovel there was no pathway cleared for him. So he had to struggle through knee-deep snow in order to reach my door! He was accompanied by an elf helper, and both of them were carrying relatively large red sacks ... that were obviously crammed full of gifts.

Once inside he sat down in a chair and allowed each of my three children to sit on his lap. In doing so, he started to pull out countless toys and treats that were meant specifically for them. And these toys and treats were *not* cheapos either! Everything was brand name, very popular toys that all the kids of the day wanted. I don't know how much everything had cost, but holy cow it had to have been a pretty penny! And *both* large bags were crammed full. Once he was finished handing out all of the gifts to my children, he stood up, turned to me and handed me a Christmas red envelope.

"And here Mom, this is for you. Have a very Merry Christmas!" Closing the door behind Santa, I was dumbfounded. I couldn't believe the outpouring of love that was just shown to us. But then, then there was the envelope that I still held in my hand. I opened it ... inside there was a grocery voucher for $150 as well as $200 cash! I was sent over into another emotional breakdown – but at least in a better form of it. It wasn't necessarily the money or grocery voucher that sent me over the edge. It was more so the lengthy poem that was written in the card itself. I don't wish to infringe on someone's copyright, so I can't quote the poem verbatim like I want to. But it basically said they knew how difficult life had been for me the last while, and that perhaps it felt like I'd never survive it; yet I had to remember that God never throws at us anymore than what we can handle. I was to remain strong, and to remember that I had tremendous support surrounding me. See, I can't even give the poem justice because of course that's not all that it says – and the poem is much more eloquent than I. But I still have that card today – after all these years. So if anyone ever asks, I'll gladly show it to them so that they can read it.

———ༀ༄ༀ———

April of 2005 and I'm still struggling financially. By this time of course Mark knew full well where I was and how terrible I was doing, but still he outright refused to pay a single cent in child support. The most that Mark would do is once a month or so call me on the phone all tanked up at one in the morning, trying to force me into having phone sex with him (which I never did comply). The only thought that I have about this behavior is that clearly he had no interest in our children; he called when of course they were all in bed sound asleep, and he wouldn't even ask how they're doing. He was just interested in finding out what color of underwear I had on.

However I still refused to go to legal aid so that I could take him to court. I just hated the idea of them putting a lien on my home! I don't know if it was pride, sheer stupidity, or perhaps my intuition telling me that going there would ultimately screw me over later on down the road – I just didn't know how other than the fact that I'd never be able to pay the lien off. No matter the reason, I wanted no part of it. Yet, I also knew that Mark was essentially digging his own grave anyways – for I knew deep down within that my children would one day look back on our trials and would question him. He would have a lot to answer to in later years.

Through these early trials though, something changed within me: I became a very defiant and angry woman who would no longer put up with *any* kind of bullshit from anyone ... and that included myself! I had enough. Enough of the struggling. Enough of the tears and fears. Enough of feeling sorry for myself. No more of that crap! I had to get up off my sorry ass and do something more for myself ... and my children. I remembered that I held ultimate power in my life – only I had the power to change things. I also needed to start nurturing myself and some of my dreams.

Over the course of the last few months, I made an acquaintance with a social worker employed with child protective services. I always had this itch within me to become involved in social work – especially child protection and family services. As my social worker friend pointed out to me: seeing as I had an extremely abusive childhood and also had the perspective of an abused wife and then single mother, I would be quite the unique social worker because I could see from the perspectives of both parent and child. He strongly supported this concept – and thus encouraged me to pursue it.

Going back to school was quite the terrifying thought. What if I ultimately failed the course? What if I'm the oldest student in the class? How am I going to afford it? How will I be able to go to school, study, work, and take care of my children all at the same time? But yet, despite those fears, the more I thought about pursuing that path, the stronger I felt a passion for it ... and the more I felt that I needed to change my life for the better and become a good role model for my three children. Furthermore, by this time my spiritual awareness had grown tremendously – to the point where I knew that if something was meant to happen, then it would happen. The only thing stopping me was me ... and my fearful human ego. Besides, I listened to my divine guidance before and it didn't steer me wrongly: I fulfilled my desire to be a homeowner ... and the results of my following that guidance were actually way beyond what I had originally expected. Who else can say they own a home with no mortgage? Some can certainly ... but not many. So I needed to listen once more. I needed to take action, but place my faith in the knowledge that Divine will come through once more ... if it's meant to be.

Through research I realized that I could apply for a government student loan. Because it was already getting rather late in the year for college applications, I immediately submitted my loan application to the government. Two weeks later I received a response in the mail: DENIED FUNDING!

My most immediate reaction was that of wanting to give up – and I felt profound anger and resentment towards Mark. Realize that in order to be accepted for a loan, well they check your credit history. Mine sucked. I had that mortgage default on there, as well as an unpaid credit card that Mark racked up (see he made me pay his credit cards off but refused to acknowledge mine) and an overdrawn bank overdraft (yes – an overdraft that was overdrawn).

After a day of once again feeling sorry for myself, I shook it off and asked for further divine guidance. Immediately I received a response from that loving voice within my mind:

"Don't give up. This is just a block that you need to overcome. You must write a letter of protest to the government. You must challenge their decision."

Okay, I thought to myself. I'll damn well challenge them all right! This time I put my anger to a more positive use: I wrote the government a seven-page letter of appeal; challenging them and explaining why I felt they should overturn their decision. I can't remember all that I wrote now, but I do recall saying something to the effect of how could I possibly make a better life for myself and my children when they wouldn't even let me? I think I basically put the blame onto them for forcing my children and I to continue living in a state of poverty.

Another two weeks pass. Then three. By the fourth week I was beginning to think they were just going to ignore me. After all, who was I kidding? Who was I anyways to challenge the government? Usually they get the final word right? But finally I received the letter: APPROVED!

Well there I had it. I was going to school that September to study social work – and the government was giving me a grand total of $23,000; which included not only the payment of my tuition and books, but also a living allowance in order to get me through the next two years.

———————

Christmas of 2005, Mark decided to show himself by coming up and staying with the children and I for a two days. He brought a few gifts for the kids, and of course plenty of beer and pot for himself. I allowed him to come for that visit simply with the hope that perhaps he would see for himself that we needed help – that I wasn't just blowing a lot of hot air about needing child support. While he did behave himself and was very polite, he still turned a blind eye to our needs.

I made a second attempt with Mark at Easter of 2006. By this time, I was exhausted with my struggles. I was to the point where once again I found myself wishing that someone would come and rescue me from my situation. Or at least get Mark to see reason and make him send me child support payments. Of course I had the government student loan to work with, but that only provided the necessities. As a matter of fact, I was so desperate by that point I almost fell for the infamous, 'I've changed. Come back to me" plea. It even got as close as me sleeping with Mark and subsequently leaving it with him that perhaps in a few months' time the children and I would reunite with him back down south. Yes, that was very stupid. I know. But in my defense I did catch myself quickly after he left.

"What the hell am I doing," I thought to myself. "I'm going to school. I have my own home that no one could ever take away from me. I am in total control over my life and everything in it. Why do I want to give that up? Just for the sake of financial security? I need to give my head a shake." I did more than that ... I made the solemn vow that never again would I subject myself, or my children, to the kind of life we had with Mark. Phew! That was a close call ... and I stood firm to my position. In fact, I also resigned myself to the idea that I would not likely ever remarry let alone live with another man. I wasn't going to give my freedom up for anything – money or no money. And Mark? No, of course he wasn't too impressed. But that was his problem ... not mine.

———— ᘓᘎᕼᕼᘎᘏ ————

The first year of my studies flew by; I worked hard and studied harder – my grades were exceptionally high (always in the high 80's to mid-90's), I would study for exams and complete assignments while having to work the psychic phone line (I'd write or read until the phone rang, do the reading, then back to studying I would go), and would clean the house and cook in between. While the children weren't in school, or if I had a particularly late class, Kevin would take care of them and made sure all was well. And, I even made a wonderful new friend at school – her name was Mary. The two of us became extremely close: helping each other with our homework, confiding in each other our troubles and desires, loaning money back and forth, and even having sleepovers once in a while. We considered each other sisters, and basically did everything together – even in the summer when school was out you would usually find us up to something together; including taking the required First Aid training course for our college studies.

Having lunch at our favorite restaurant and dreading having to go back to the first aid class, Mary and I started talking about what kinds of goals we expected to fulfill in the upcoming school year. Of course I had to express my passionate desire to get back into my horses. I know it had nothing to do with school, but the way I looked at it my goal to get a horse would somehow be fulfilled through my schooling. So it was related in a way. Well, what Mary said next changed the course of my entire life:

"Hey! I have a friend who wants to sell her horse." I was so shocked and excited I actually choked on my coffee.

"What?" I yelled. Ooopsies – I yelled so loud that everyone else in the restaurant turned to look at me to see what the hell my issue was. "What breed of horse? How old? Is it a mare or gelding or stallion?" And just as importantly, how much?"

"Lisa I'm not a horse person," Mary smiled. "I have no clue about anything. After class we'll head over to your place and I'll give her a call. Okay?"

Well okie dokie pokie! And that's exactly what we did. Actually, we did one even better: right after Mary called her friend, we took a taxi out to see her and her horse. I didn't want to say anything to Mary, but without even seeing the horse, I already had it in my mind that it was mine.

We pulled up into the driveway and immediately I spot my beauty: a very sturdy and stunning four year old paint quarter horse mare. Apache was her name, and she had just given birth to a pretty little foal only three months prior. It took me a mere second to fall in love with Apache. I didn't hesitate in discussing the payment particulars with Mary's friend: I would pay a little bit right away, and then the rest when the second half of my government student loan was issued. Done deal! She even agreed to allow me to board Apache at her place for $100 a month – as I didn't actually have anywhere else to go.

I could see the wisdom and gentle love in her eyes ... yet there was also something about her that troubled me. Could she have suffered some form of abuse or neglect? I couldn't shake off that distinct nervous energy coming from her, but to be honest I believe it just solidified my desire to buy her. Apache was mine. That's all there was to it. We were two souls who had similar backgrounds coming together as one.

And it certainly didn't take long for an extremely strong bond to form between the two of us. It was clear that she would never intentionally hurt me (one day she spooked and bucked me very hard off into a steel fence post – thus dislocating my shoulder. You should have seen the look on her face. She felt horrible!). Yet I had witnessed her almost running over her previous owner! Apache also adored children: There were many days where I would be riding and training her inside the round pen. She would do wonderful and listen perfectly ... until she heard my girls laughing or talking. She would come to a dead halt even from a fast canter (which I had to be prepared for otherwise I'd end up going up over her head!) and look for them. She wouldn't listen to a single thing I tried to tell her to do ... she just wanted to see the girls. So I'd give in and walk her up to the fence where the girls would be standing and watching, she'd let them pet her, feed her a few handfuls of grass, and would even bow down to them gracefully (Apache was trained where if you touched her left front knee she would lift up her leg and put her head down to the ground).

I now had a true companion and loving spirit in Apache, and I once again began to feel like finally my life was working out as it should. I was excited for the first time since moving to Iroquois Falls, and all I could do was look forward at the prospective future in eager anticipation.

———·······———

"Lisa, I'm so sorry but my boyfriend doesn't want you to bring your kids here. I don't know why – they're so cute and well-behaved. He said that you can come but you can't bring them." I couldn't believe what I was hearing. How could she do this to me?

"Listen, if I go somewhere then you're damn right my children would be accompanying me!" I bellowed. "What right does he have anyways? You're going to let him control what you say and do? I made that mistake myself with my ex ... it's not a good path to walk down."

"I know," the woman replied. I could tell that she had been crying, and it was clear that she really didn't want me to stop boarding Apache with her. "But it's his property after all. So what can I say? But Lisa he said that if you won't do that, then you have to take Apache somewhere else."

"Lisa," Mary whispered. She had been sitting there listening to the entire conversation all that time. "Don't worry. We'll figure something out. I don't know what her problem is or why she is treating you like this, but I don't like it. And we will work this out I promise you." Nodding my head to acknowledge Mary, I sighed deeply and resigned myself to the fact that yet once again more chaos to deal with. It just felt like every time I turned around something else comes up and kicks me a good one.

"All right," I said to the woman. "I'll see what I can do. I will get Apache out of there as soon as I figure out what I'm doing." I was so upset and angry I didn't even say good-bye. I just slammed down the phone and burst into tears.

"Lisa please don't cry," Mary put her arm around me to comfort me. "Listen, I know some guy that could maybe help. Get me the phone book and I'll see if I can find his phone number. He's really super nice. I'm sure if he can't help he will at least be able to give us a suggestion or two." I hand Mary the phone book and she flips through the pages, madly scanning for 'this guy's' number.

"Ah ha! I got it. Gimme that phone!" I couldn't say a word. I was speechless as I just felt helplessly lost. I silently handed her the phone and watched as she dialed the number. Someone answered,

"Hey! This is Mary. How are you?" There was a momentary pause as Mary listened to the voice on the other end. Once they were done she immediately went right into pleading our case.

"Tell him that I'll do anything he wants if he can help me," I begged. "Just so long as it isn't sex." Yes, even in anger or upset I tend to try and throw in some of my warped sense of humor. I think it worked though because I vaguely heard a man's laugh and Mary say,

"Oh God thank you so much. You'll be here in an hour? Great I'll let her know. Thank you again. It means so much to both of us." Mary then turned to me, "Go get ready. He's on his way. Don't worry about the kids. I'll get them supper and stay here until you get back."

It wasn't even a full hour when I spot a navy blue Chevy truck pull up in my back alley. Behind it was a brown horse trailer with large yellow lettering on the sides that said, 'Ti-Caz.' I raced across the yard, swung the passenger door open and leapt inside. I turned to this wonderful good Samaritan in a man,

"Thank you so ….." I stopped in mid-sentence. It was cowboy man from Canada Day two years ago! Remember him? I sure as hell did … but clearly he didn't know me from Adam. In realizing who he was, I completely forgot to finish my sentence. Thankfully I don't think he even noticed.

"Oh you are so welcome," he smiled. There was that amazing French accent again! "What's your name again? I'm sorry; I'm horrible at remembering names. One too many concussions you know. My name is Martial, but everyone just calls me Caz. Now where is your horse? Let's get her the hell out of there. She'll be in good hands at my ranch I promise you."

———ᘯᘯᘯᘯᘯ———

Martial loaded Apache into his trailer without incident; except for a few brief nervous moments where Apache, clearly not understanding what was happening, looked over at me wild-eyed as if begging me to stop this man from loading her into the trailer. I noticed that about her: she definitely didn't like men for some reason.

Driving with Apache to his ranch, Martial went on to explain to me that not only had he been a horse trainer for most of his life, he was actually Apache's original owner! He was shocked at her behavior with him – she was never shy or hard to work with. However, he did in fact confirm that poor Apache had been beaten on numerous occasions by that woman's boyfriend (the one that 'kicked me and my children off his property') – where on one occasion he actually whacked her in the head with a shovel. He had tried to get Apache back and out of there, but obviously he was unsuccessful. So he expressed his deepest respect and gratitude towards me for being her new owner, and that he would help me work with her to get her straightened around once more. Until then, he advised it not wise to ride her without supervision. Not just because she had clearly been abused, but also because when she was underhandedly taken from Martial by that girl, Apache was just barely green-broke (which means basically she just had her ground basics and hadn't been ridden enough). You just never knew what she'd do – she was still way too unpredictable. Given the fact that she spooked a month prior and dislocated my shoulder, how could I argue?

The Journey Part Three:
New Relationships and Marriage

———————— ⧉ ————————

*F*rom September to December of 2006, every weekend I would take the $20 taxi drive out to Martial's (Caz's) ranch to work with Apache. In doing so I finally got to know him more, as well as Chinook, Chevy, and Apache's twin sister Cheyenne. I learned very quickly that he had a rather quirky sense of humor and was quite the good story-teller; so good in fact that he had my children believing that he had a bear cub living in the crawl space underneath the house (which was a ramshackle of a house may I add: it had one bedroom, a very small living area, no actual flooring other than the rough plywood underlay, it heated with a wood stove, and in the winter it was so cold in there that you had to have that fire stoked full blast just so the pipes wouldn't freeze). Martial absolutely adored children; he had two young boys of his own – which ironically were pretty much the same ages as my three children. He was a very fun and interesting man to spend time with; always had unique ideas on fun activities for the children and he had a heart of gold where he would do anything for anyone. I formed quite the strong friendship with him over the few months I boarded Apache there. And I do believe he felt the same, for he even trusted me enough to ask me to help him do some Christmas shopping for his two boys. It turned out that we had quite a bit in common; except for one thing: Martial certainly had the strong addiction to pot. It didn't bother me too much – I was quite used to it after all. Just so long as he didn't smoke in front of my children ... that's all that mattered. And he never did either.

At this stage in my life I felt very comfortable with myself and where I was at. I was happy and free, and not even thinking about looking for (or even needing for that matter) another man in my life. I was on my own for two and a half years, and finally had established a general direction and routine for myself. I had begun my second year in my social work studies, and with the help of my government student loan my financial worries were greatly alleviated to the point where I was no longer in debt with the utilities. To make things even better, my work at the online psychic website doubled; where I was then actually able to save a few hundred dollars each pay.

I had Apache, I made a few new good friends, I was breezing through my college studies with flying colors, I always had food in the house, and my children were thriving. The future was starting to look much more exciting – and for once I was eagerly looking forward to it. Yes, there were days when I felt somewhat lonely and yearned for companionship. But for the most part, I realized that I didn't need it ... I didn't need it to survive and I didn't need 'saving.' And that was a huge step for me because for many years I believed that I couldn't do it alone – that I needed that man in my life to feel whole and capable. Over those two years I had proven to myself that it was the furthest thing from the truth. I *was* strong. I *was* capable. And I didn't need someone else to handle anything for me.

I was a true warrior, and I knew that I would eventually rise to the top. I just had to keep going.

———∾∿⟋⟋⟍⟍∿∾———

One frigid winter Friday afternoon in January of 2007, Mary and I just sat down to begin our sociology class when Mary, wide-eyed and clearly full of excited energy turned to me and gasped,

"Oh my God. Lisa, did you hear what happened?"

"Huh?" Of course I was clueless. "What do you mean? What are you talking about?"

"Shit Lisa it's all over town!" Mary began. "Caz was in a major accident with one of the horses last night."

"What?!" I jumped out of my chair in sheer panic and concern. "What happened? Where is he? Is he in the hospital here in town or somewhere else? I have to go to him. Oh my god!"

"I don't know a darn thing other than that," Mary said. "But if anyone knows anything it would be George – he was the one that found him." Mary was still talking ... but I went running. I raced the entire way home; the adrenaline was pumping so hard that the -40C temperature didn't even seem to fizz on my asthma like it usually did. Little did I know, poor Mary was chasing after me – I didn't realize until I reached my back door and I heard a heavy huffing and puffing coming from behind.

I sped through the phone book, found George's number, and got on the phone – by this time of course my classes for the day are completely forgotten. Thankfully George was home; he told me what had happened, what he saw when he found Martial, and where Martial currently was.

Martial was still here in the hospital, but was in serious condition. He had gone out to feed and water the horses after he arrived home rather late from his shift at work. However, he was in quite the rush doing so as he realized that his yellow lab Sheba was in the process of giving birth to a litter of puppies. So "spooky" horses were the furthest thing from his mind in those moments – for he wanted to be there for Sheba throughout the birthing process.

He had entered into the large stall located at the rear of the barn – where Apache and her sister Cheyenne stayed. He opened the door, and just as he hurriedly reached up to turn on the light above his head, that's when he got it: one of the horses kicked him square in the face. Down Martial went – with the door then wide open, an anxiety-stricken Apache and her sister walked over his semi-conscious body, out the main doors of the barn and into the yard.

Thankfully, Martial had requested that George come out to the ranch to bring him a few bales of hay.

That was when George found him. As George relates the story, he says to this day that it was something straight out of a horror movie: somehow Martial had managed to drag himself to his still-running truck (which we are all so grateful for because that night the temperature reached a whopping -45C). That was where he ultimately passed out. Blood everywhere, Martial was almost totally unrecognizable; his jaw was shattered and his left eye had popped out of its socket and was just dangling on his cheek.

As George filled me in on all the details, only three things ran through my mind: I had to get to Martial, I was going to take care of the ranch for him, and god almighty it was Apache that kicked him. I thanked George for everything, informed him that I was heading to the hospital straight away, and that I would stay at the ranch over the weekend.

With Mary by my side as I saw Martial in the hospital ... I couldn't help but break down into tears. George was right; he was almost completely unrecognizable. His entire head had swollen ten times its normal size, he had two black eyes (thankfully the emergency medical team on staff that night were able to place his left eye back into place), and he could barely speak due to the broken jaw. I gently took his hand and sat beside him on his bed, apologizing to no end and telling him to not worry about the ranch – that both George and I would take care of everything. I cannot remember what else I had said, but as I went to leave I bent over and carefully kissed him on his forehead. I wished him safe travels (as they had to airlift him to a specialized hospital in Toronto), and that I would see him as soon as he got back. All Martial could do was weakly (and crookedly) smile, give my hand a gentle squeeze, and mumble 'thank you dear.'

The moment I arrived at the farm I immediately went out to check on all of the horses (at that time there were eight total). Now, usually Apache would come galloping up to the fence the moment she either heard me or spotted me, and nine times out of ten an argument would break out between her and Chinook – the two of them always vied for my attention. Not this time. This time, Apache hung back away from the rest of the herd. No matter how much I tried to coax her to come see me, she just stood there and stared at me longingly. Her energy (and body language) immediately told me that I had been right. There was no denying it: Apache had been the one that kicked Martial in the face.

———✦———

After Martial had reconstructive surgery on his face and jaw, he was unable to work or do any amount of lifting for a good three months. As a result, I would go out to the farm every other day or so just to help him with the caretaking of the horses and chores inside the house. Because he couldn't work, he obviously didn't have much of an income either. So I tried to help the best I could by paying extra for Apache's board, loaned him some money to pay his rent and hydro, and I even helped out by buying one of Sheba's puppies.

A mere month after his accident, it seemed our connection took on an entirely new energy ... a more romantic energy. I remember rushing through my social work placement just so that I could be with him on Valentine's Day. I would even blow off whole days for my placement just to go out to the ranch and spend time with him. No, I know that wasn't the best of ideas – we teach our children to not skip school yet there I was doing the same damn thing. But you tend to do stupid things when you're truly in love.

And that was huge for me: being in true love. I never in my life felt the way that I did when I was with Martial ... not even when I first met Mark (and if you recall I was fifteen when I met him)! Even when Martial and I were apart – I would just think about him and I would get those crazy butterflies in my stomach (of which up until then I always thought it was silliness when people talked about them. Well, I certainly got a taste of it for myself! And it definitely wasn't silliness). I even found myself wondering about the potential future: would he be in it? Where was this going to go? I actually had a mix of different emotions because on one hand I felt like that 'silly teenage-girl-puppy-love butterflies,' but yet on the other hand the more mature and wise part of me would question what the heck I was doing – what happened to the 'I'm a warrior and don't need anybody' attitude? I started to see so many of my clients within my own self – I had the same questions, the same concerns. Yet for some stupid reason, I couldn't help myself the way that

I had helped countless folks for so many years. I couldn't answer my own darn questions. Or at least so I thought.

I finally reached a point where I tried to adopt the attitude of 'whatever will be, will be.' I had to stop myself from projecting into the future – I had to live in the moment as each moment came. Besides, that's literally all one could ever do anyways!

———∽◦◦◦◦◦◦◦◦———

"Where the heck is Martial," I questioned Mary. "Have you heard from him at all? I haven't seen or heard tell of him for a week now. That's not like him. Usually he calls me every other day or so. I've tried calling the ranch and I just get the answering machine every time."

"I don't know," Mary replied. "Maybe call George to see if he knows anything." So call George I did. And what he told me somewhat upset me ... but who was I at that point? Martial had gone into detox and rehab for his pot addiction; he would be away for two more weeks. Really?! Seriously?! Why did he not inform me of this, I thought to myself. I knew that he was thinking about it – he talked about the possibility of it with me not all that long ago. He should have at least told me that he was going for pete sake! Quickly shoving my upset aside (as again I'll say it – who was I to get upset like that?), I thanked George for the information and informed him that in a few days, when my school week was over, I would head out to the farm to give him a break.

Darn men, I thought to myself. So inconsiderate of others. Ugh!

* Little did I know that Martial had no choice but to up and leave right away: he received the call that they had a bed available, but he had to leave literally right then. Hence why he didn't call me to tell me – he just didn't have the time to do so (nor the mindset). Martial actually called me the moment he returned from rehab and apologized.

———ⴑⴑⴑⴑ———

Not even two days after I had spoken to George, and literally the day before I could get out to the farm, we caught word that there had been a serious chimney fire out at the ranch. I do not know enough to say how the fire had started, but all I do know is that poor Martial had one hell of a mess to come home to. And it wasn't just because of the massive damage from the chimney fire either ... little did we know that behind closed doors a secret deal was going down: someone bought the farm from the owner (and that was after Martial himself put in an offer to buy it). Upon Martial's return home, we learned that he had only one month to find another farm ... or else sell all the horses and move into town. This was *not* a very good situation; especially for a new addict in recovery.

Both Martial and I tried tirelessly to search for a new farm to move to, but we ultimately came up dry. There was nothing available, and Martial refused to board at someone else's farm. As heartbreaking as it was for both of us, we had no choice but to sell all of the horses. That was ultimately the hardest thing that Martial had to do: and to this day if you ask him to talk about this he will shed tears and will say that he doesn't really wish to talk about it. All horses were sold except Apache. At the time, Apache was pregnant by Martial's stallion Diamond – and I wanted to try and hold on for as long as I could as I wished to try and at least keep the baby (as the baby essentially represented a combining of my spirit and Martial's spirit). So Martial found a beautiful farm where I could board her (and her baby once born). As for Martial, I had offered that he come stay with me. But he just didn't like that idea for whatever reason ... which was fine. So he rented a small apartment in town. However, because it was an apartment, he wasn't able to keep both of his yellow labs with him. Therefore I took Sheba (she too was pregnant once more) and he kept his male Max.

Neither Martial or Max were too thrilled about having to live in town ... especially in a closed-in, small two bed-room apartment. But that's okay ... because it would become apparent relatively quickly that they wouldn't be staying there for very long.

———∿∿∽⌒⊙⌒⊙⌒⊙∽∿∿———

June 1, 2007, Martial handed me a beautiful bouquet of red roses and sat down at my kitchen table. I loved that about him. He was always full of pleasant surprises and showed huge gestures of love in the smallest of ways.

"Well," Martial began. Hmmm ... I didn't like his tone. I knew him well enough by that time that I knew whatever he was about to say wasn't going to be the best of news. "I have some bad news. I have to move. They sold the apartment and everyone has to get out. We all have a month."

"Holy crap! As if. You just moved there," I was beside myself with shock. It just seemed that if it weren't for bad luck, we just wouldn't have any luck at all. "What are you going to do? Where are you going to go now?" After a few minutes pause and a brief glance down at the floor as if somewhat ashamed of himself, Martial leaned over the table and whispered,

"Well, I guess I'll be moving in with you my dear. That is, if you'll have me." Without a second's hesitation I welcomed him into my world. And not a day goes by that I ever regret having made that decision.

———

Of course the moment Martial moved in, my children's and my world drastically changed. All of a sudden we found ourselves operating like a traditional family. Those months were the happiest and most peaceful any of us had ever experienced. Martial brought a love and light into our world that we didn't even know existed. Not a day went by where we didn't laugh or show love to one another.

By this point, Mark was of course outraged at the thought that there I was – involved with another man and allowing another man around my children. Did that outrage finally make him step up to the plate though? Not a chance. If anything, I believe it just pushed him further away from his responsibilities as a father. For me, what I had picked up from Mark's energy, it was an attitude of, "Good. Now that she has another man, he can take care of the kids. I've gotten off the hook." And later on it would seem apparent that I was rather accurate with that particular observation.

Christmas Day of 2007, Martial and I made a delicious turkey dinner and invited his mother, sister, nephew and a close friend of his family to join us. Martial also had an announcement to make to his family:

Earlier that Christmas morning, Martial proposed to me ... and I said 'yes.'

* I unfortunately botched Martial's marriage proposal (leave it to me right?). I had bought Martial a brand new 12-string guitar and presented it to him first thing that morning. But poor Martial – he felt so horrible: there I had given him this gorgeous guitar, meanwhile all he presented me with was a 'silly' coffee maker. He felt so terrible that he went out to his truck where he had stashed my engagement ring – his plan was he was going to actually propose to me in front of his family, by getting down on one knee and all! He came back in and handed me the neatly wrapped box. I knew what it was the moment I opened it up, and without even saying a word I hugged him tightly and started to cry. Martial too started to cry ... but why is beyond me. Perhaps you can ask him?

August of 2008 – literally one week before our wedding and all was set for the ceremony: dress was in, all the arrangements for the reception confirmed, decorations and guest favors all ready to go, invitations long been sent out to guests ... I received an email from the folks where I was boarding Apache. We were to have the actual ceremony on their ranch – and I was to ride Apache into the ceremony itself, with little Serene (Apache's baby) following close behind.

Well not anymore. The email informed me that they no longer wanted us to have the wedding at their ranch. I broke into hysterics. What the hell are we going to do now? Everything was ready to go! There was only one week left! One week! How could they do that to us? We were having problems with those people for a few months prior, but we never thought in a million years that something this low would be put upon us. But it was ... and we had to deal with it ... and pronto. As if Martial could sense that something was wrong, not even five minutes after reading the email he called me from work. I don't think I ever felt such angry energy coming from him than what I did in those moments.

"Don't worry, babe." He tried to hide his anger from me, but that doesn't work too well with me being such a strong empath. "Bastards. We'll straighten this out I promise you. I'll handle it. No worries and no more tears."

Everyone: Martial, his mother and sister, our friend George, myself, and even the town, worked together to ensure that we had the best wedding imaginable. Countless phone calls and last minute preparations were made, when finally the big day arrived.

Even though it had been raining all day, the rain actually stopped just for the ceremony itself. Martial and I rode two of George's horses into the ceremony, and we had all five of our children recite a poem or passage from the Bible. Where was the wedding held? Well, this didn't occur to me until much later on, but our wedding took place in the exact same park where I had met Martial so very briefly on that Canada Day four years prior.

Totally unplanned ... but all worked out exactly the way it was supposed to – and exactly how Divine had intended all along.

Lessons Learned & Guidance
to Follow: Finding Paradise

———————— ❦ ————————

*A*s I had mentioned very early on in this book, I learned a tremendous amount of lessons and received the most astounding divine guidance in respect to my past relationship – especially at the end and most certainly once I got out on my own. The reason for telling my story is to inspire, motivate, and teach others how they too can rebuild themselves after having gone through a toxic relationship. However, I have to say that over the many years of my working in the metaphysical field, I have given this same exact guidance to countless individuals who were just having a hard time looking for that very special someone. And indeed, I've likewise received many letters from them to let me know that they had reached their relationship goals successfully. So everyone can benefit from the guidance that's about to be given – and they are strongly encouraged to at least give it a go!

In the following pages you will find very important steps or lessons and divine spiritual guidance to remember (and thus implement) along your own relationship path. Again, these insights are for everyone to use – and the majority of them are to be used simultaneously with one another.

Create Change Before Divine Steps In

This particular piece of guidance is geared more towards those individuals who are 'stuck' in a relationship or situation that they do not want to stay in – but are still there for whatever reason.

Not one single person even bothers to consider changing an aspect or two in their lives if they're comfortable and happy. Right? We only desire change whenever we're miserable and feeling unfulfilled in some way. We have to experience some level of discomfort before we take action for ourselves. However, some of us (like myself) can be rather stubborn in getting our butts in gear – mainly for one of two reasons: 1. Because we hold a specific belief system or two that causes us to hold on (i.e. staying in a toxic marriage for the sake of the children or divorce goes against religious beliefs), and 2. Because we are fearful of the change itself and the unknown. We know that we're unhappy and we know that we need to make changes, but we become somewhat paralyzed by these fears and beliefs. As a result, we can hang in there for quite the indeterminate amount of time. But Divine hates this. In fact, It can't stand it! Indeed Divine has a tremendous amount of patience and tries to allow us to learn and grow in our own due course and time. However, It will eventually reach a point where patience is no longer an option – as was in my case.

If you don't take action for yourself, Divine *can* step in to try and *force* the change to occur. And nine times out of ten, if and when that happens, unfortunately the situation proves to be much more intense and chaotic than what it would have been if you had just taken action yourself.

A purpose of being here on this earthly plane is to learn and grow – which *usually* we are all constantly doing whether we realize it or not. It is also divinely intended that we experience happiness and fulfillment. But in a situation such as this, we stop growing and we are constantly in some amount of turmoil (and the levels of unhappiness deepen as time goes on – it just gets worse and worse). This is why Divine eventually steps in – in this situation the unhappiness and impeded growth is grossly prolonged. Therefore Divine says, "Okay, enough is enough! You've done enough damage to yourself!" And like a volcano that's been building up pressure over two or three decades, the situation explodes into quite the destructive eruption.

This happened with me. Divine stepped in so that I would be forced to make those changes in my life – and indeed it was much more chaotic and severe a situation than what it would have been if I had only listened to my heart, pushed aside the fears and just moved. If I had simply told Mark that I was leaving the marriage, of course he wouldn't have been too impressed and I likely would have had to deal with some sort of fight. But that would have been the end of it. Instead, I held on; paralyzed by fear of the unknown. As a result, I became stagnant in my spiritual growth and wasn't fulfilling my purpose of experiencing happiness and fulfillment – which led Divine into creating one of the most traumatic experiences I've ever gone through in my marriage: The Night of Reckoning.

If you feel unhappy, unfulfilled, and a yearning to 'escape' from the situation, that is your first clue that you need to take action and create change. It's certainly not something you wish to procrastinate on. It will just get worse as time passes. And I really don't think I need to state just how serious of a situation it is when one is involved in an abusive relationship like I had been.

Have Patience With Yourself and Your Processes

There are two different concepts that need to be discussed in this particular piece of advice.

Everyone has different priorities and trains of focus – which of course do change over the course of any given life path. For example, some folks prefer to just focus on their careers and build themselves financially. Other folks wish to just work on themselves in some way – for example emotional growth and healing from a traumatic childhood or relationship. Whatever the case is, it doesn't really matter. The point is everyone has different sets of priorities at any given time in their lives.

So for those of you who have overly concerned parents and/or well-meaning friends who keep trying to force you into having a relationship – you need to tell them as gently as possible to bugger off! Of course they love you and only want the best for you. That's why they're pressuring you so much. But the thing is only *you* know what is good for you and what you want for yourself in your life. You can't force a person into a relationship! A person will pursue a relationship when *they* are ready for one. So the advice here is to not listen to anyone who's trying to force you into doing something that you feel you are not ready for. You must listen to yourself, and your own heart and spirit. What *you* want for yourself and your life is the most important ... not the desires of others.

What goes hand in hand with the above is the concept of you needing patience with yourself and your own processes; especially when you're just getting out of a rather significant relationship. Realize that whenever we end a relationship, we go through an actual grieving process. We grieve for the loss itself, for what was, for what could have been, for what we wished might have been, and so on. Even in coming out of the most abusive of relationships, a grieving process will still occur. It is a process very similar in nature to that of when one of our beloved family members or friends pass over to the other side. We go through all of the five stages: denial, anger, bargaining, depression, and acceptance. We go through those stages back and forth, and everyone is different where they experience each stage for different lengths of time. You cannot rush these stages, nor can you force yourself to feel any differently than what you are currently.

I have to admit that this process itself is the number one reason why I tend to disagree with the common belief that there is a set "time limit" between relationships. For example, some hold the belief that if a person got out of a relationship that lasted for fourteen years, then it would take them seven years to be ready for a new relationship. In other words, it takes the person approximately half of the time the relationship lasted in order to be 'ready' for a new love partner. That's hogwash! My previous marriage to Mark lasted fourteen years, but it only took me three and a half years to connect with Martial. There is really no set time limit! It all depends on the person, their desires, and most certainly their spirit and how aware they are spiritually and emotionally.

Going through the grief process is also quite the growth and change process in itself. It changes you emotionally and spiritually – so you will never be the same person that you once were. As a result, when you do near the end of the process you will need time to re-learn who you are – to become acquainted with and deeply know the new you. This too cannot be rushed.

Take your time, and don't listen to anyone else but yourself (as long as you're not listening to the fearful human ego that is). You will eventually reach a point of true and permanent acceptance – and you will know exactly when you are there and ready to move forward once more.

Ignore & Overcome Fears

The human ego loves to trap us with as many fears as it possibly can: What if I'm always going to be alone? What if I can't survive financially if I leave the relationship? What if I just find another 'loser' of a partner? What if I can't afford to go to school or actually fail? What if, what if, what if. Stop that! Stop those swirling 'what if' questions – that's the fearful human ego trying to mess around with you. Also stop the who's, where's, why's, and how's, as well as the I can't, I won't, and I don't. They just don't help. They're all fear-based questions and statements that truly don't serve you. Yes of course it's good to question – that's just a part of logical planning. But the trick is to not dwell on those questions! If you're dwelling, again it is your ego at work instead of your spirit and heart.

Listen, if we always allowed our fears to get the best of us, ultimately we would *never* accomplish *anything* in our lives! Furthermore, the more we focus on our fears and allow them to dictate what we can and cannot do, then we unfortunately just attract more things to be fearful of. We will discuss this particular concept in a few moments; it is all about the Law of Attraction.

Push aside the ego and its fears – do not allow it to tell you what you can and can't do! You can do *anything* that you set your heart and mind to. Sure, sometimes we may have to go through some rough waters along the way. But we get through it, coming out stronger than before, and closer to our destinations and goals. Just do what you have to do – no matter how scary it might seem to you at first. If you want something to change ... then go for it and do what you must. After all, you will never know just how strong and capable you truly are if you don't start off by putting one foot in front of the other and determinedly move forward on your path ... as you should. Don't allow yourself to fall into that nasty "I can't," trap or the "I'm going back to the ex because at least it's familiar territory," either. That's your fear trying to gain a firm hold over you – and your ego trying to make you believe that you can't make it on your own. I came way too darn close to falling into that myself; I was so tired of being the single parent struggling to survive every day that I came within inches of returning to my ex-husband. But then I remembered how much I had actually accomplished. I wasn't about to give all that up – not for anything in the world. However, I also forced myself to remember exactly *why* I left that relationship to begin with. I would constantly go through re-runs of all the nasty episodes that I endured. Everything that was said to me and everything that had ever been done to me; all of my memories of those horrible past experiences would play back like a never-ending movie in my mind. Did I want to go back to that? No way! Once I came to that solid conclusion, I would then feel all of those negative emotions come flooding back into my heart: the anger, the resentment, and the disgust. As a result of feeling those emotions all over again, I actually regained tremendous levels of determination, inner strength, self-respect, and certainty.

So I would have to also add here that this is an excellent time to put those negative emotions and energy to good use. A lot of people might disagree with my suggestion to focus on and utilize emotions such as anger and resentment. That's all right – those folks just have a different way and belief. But those are two of the most powerful emotions known to be in existence (I wouldn't use hate so much though – as there is a strong element there of wishing harm towards another ... which in turn creates an instant karmic connection that you really do not want to have). And you *can* use negative emotions and turn them into more positive ones! So why not use some of the most powerful negative emotions in order to create some of the most powerfully positive emotions and outcomes? Just so long as your main goal is for your highest good and doesn't involve or harm that past partner; which in this case would indeed be that of greater determination, strength and self-respect for yourself. So if you find yourself getting close to the point where I was at, force yourself to remember why you left that past relationship – and use the negative emotions that those memories create in order to fuel your fire. It works!

Don't Idly Wait for Miracles

Well, this one somewhat goes with ignoring fears and creating change – but with a small addition:

no amount of prayers will help you if you don't put actual physical work into trying to fulfill goals.

Of course all prayers are heard – and yes granted some of them are in fact fulfilled without us doing too much. However, when it comes to relationships we *must* take some sort of physical action. I mean, that's just being realistic right? You're not going to meet your intended life partner if you're sitting on your butt watching television all day and night – that is unless your water pipes burst or your fuse box shorts out – in which case you'll need to contact a plumber or electrician and hope that they're you're intended one. I'm sorry for the slight sarcastic humor, but this is a rut that many folks seem to fall into … and then they don't understand why their prayers aren't being answered! You need to take definitive action in order for anything to happen. Nothing is just going to 'magically' drop into your lap or knock on your doorstep. I know that's a rather harsh and blunt thing to say, but it's just a cold hard fact.

Something to remember – and this goes for anything in life whether it's finding that special relationship or manifesting that dream job: we do need to pray and make positive affirmations. But our relationship with Divine is the very same as what it is with any living person: it is a 50-50 two-way street in terms of effort in order for the connection to be truly successful. We have to meet Divine in the middle – and give Divine the tools that It needs in order to help us actually reach our specific goals. If you hire a carpenter to build you a set of kitchen cabinets, how can he build them if you don't first supply him with the lumber? Nothing can be created out of thin air. Us taking physical action automatically gives Divine what It needs in order to fulfill Its 'share' of the required effort of work. I know what you're asking yourself at this point: What kind of action do I take then? Well, I shall be coming to all of that next. Taking physical action involves all of the following: asking for help and direction from your guides, following your guidance, self-love, pursuing interests, changing how and what you search for, and utilizing the Law of Attraction.

Ask for Help & Direction From Your Angels and Guides

In my story, you may recall how I said that it was almost as if I was waiting for someone to come along to save me – to whisk me away from the entire situation and take me to a safe haven. Of course I was looking for a physical being ... a knight in shining armor so to speak. Even throughout my trials as a single parent I would silently pray for help and direction – and to be 'saved'. A few of the worst feelings in the world is that of feeling at a sheer loss, helplessness and powerlessness – of not knowing which end is up, what to do, or what direction to travel.

It is true that the only beings or persons that can 'save' us in the end are ourselves. However, all of us have unconditionally loving and wise help and direction ... and it comes from our angels and guides.

Our angels and guides are always with us. They are there to help guide us. But the catch is that pretty much every single guide and angel will not step in until we specifically ask them to! They will not interfere unless we request it.

You can ask your angels and guides for guidance simply by praying either in your mind or aloud – whatever your preference ... and then be very aware and observant over the following days for subtle signs and messages that they will try to give you. These signs and messages can come in any form: hearing a specific song on the radio, seeing a road sign with a rather 'oddball' message that resonates with you somehow, a book falling from a shelf and opening to a certain page, or here's one that I'll give you that's very personal in nature – from my own life: When I first started dating Martial, I was very skeptical and was constantly questioning myself if it was the right thing to be doing at that time ... if I was on the intended path and if Martial was who I should be focusing on. Out of the blue one day, while Martial was working out in the barn with the horses, I came across an old letter sitting on a small wooden table that he had in the kitchen. I didn't know why I felt the need to pick it up and read it – I thought I was just being a nosey parker. That was until I saw what the letter was about. The letter was dated for the year 1997, and it was from a certain collection agency on behalf of a credit card with an outstanding amount owing. The letter itself may not sound too significant to you right now, but it will in a second: The year I saw this letter it was 2007 – ten years from the date it was originally written (what was a ten year old letter doing out and in such plain view?), the collection agency as well as the credit card were both exactly the same as what I had dealt with the prior year – same agency and same credit card. And the real kicker: it was for the same amount owing! How's that for a sign! It confirmed for me that yes, I was on the right path and that all was going to work out. As time passed, I quickly likewise learned that there were rather uncanny correlations with names between my family and Martial's: my one daughter's first name is his mother's middle name, one of his brother's first names is the male version of my other daughter's first name, I have an uncle named Martial of whom I've never met, and one of his sister's first names is my middle name. It may sound like coincidence to a lot of folks – but it spoke volumes for me. Therefore, in paying attention to signs from your own guides, keep that in mind: it will speak volumes to you even though your explanation or reasoning to others may look like total coincidence or hogwash. Divine signs from our angels and guides are very personal in nature – but they may not always be as 'in your face' as what some of mine were (I'm just too stubborn and dumb, so I was always going to my guides looking for help – that's why I received such strong validation ha ha! I think I made quite the pest of myself).

With that being said, one of the absolute best methods to communicate with your guides and ask for assistance is via meditation and visualization techniques. The reason why I suggest this method is because you will get to meet your angel or guide 'face to face' (spiritually-speaking if you know what I mean) and have actual conversations with them.

When you meet your guides or angels – and do so on a regular basis – you develop a very powerful connection between you ... thus even creating the potential to receive some of those 'in your face' signs like myself.

Many years ago I wrote an article outlining how to meet animal totem guides and included my own very special meditation/visualization technique. I have referred hundreds of different people to this particular meditation, and almost all have given feedback to say that they were ultimately very successful in meeting not just their animal guides but also angels, human spirit guides, spirits of deceased loved ones, and other celestial beings. I shall include that very same meditation/visualization at the end of this book for you to use.

Then pay attention to the messages received – not just in your meditation but in the physical world as well. Be alert ... and just as importantly give thanks when they're noticed and follow through with them! There's no point asking for guidance if you're not going to listen and take that advice.

Listen To & Follow Your Intuition and Divine Guidance

In addition to asking for and paying attention to all of those signs of guidance from your angels and guides, you likewise need to listen to and follow through with your own intuition and guidance from Higher Self (which in many instances can actually be your guides and angels working though that particular 'channel').

Guidance from this level will come across as a 'silent knowing' or even sometimes a seemingly impulsive reaction. Or you feel like you should say or do a certain thing but have absolutely no clue why; like in the case of me picking up that collection agency's letter. Another example of the infamous 'silent knowing' was when I put my bid in for my home purchase. I didn't know why I felt the need to say the amount that I did; I just 'knew' that I needed to stick to that amount because I wanted the negotiations to be over as smoothly and quickly as possible. There were actually many different examples of this level of guidance in my story, including when I just 'knew' that I needed to move north, when my friend Mary took me to see my horse for the first time, and when I felt the strong desire to write that 7-page letter of appeal to the government in an attempt to overturn their decision to deny my student loan application.

The trick to following this guidance (or any type of spiritual guidance for that matter) though is to not ever second-guess or question yourself. Try to not even give it a second thought. Despite the fear and despite the strong urge to let the human ego over-analyze and negatively talk you down, just do it. Usually your most initial thought and/or impulse and/or reaction is what you should actually be focusing and thus working on.

Nurture Yourself: Self Love & Pursuing Interests

It is true the saying that you cannot love another until you first love yourself. You love yourself by taking good and proper care of your entire being – which of course involves that of you taking care of yourself health-wise by exercising, eating and sleeping proper, and so on. It also includes that of watching the negative self-talk – which means needing to strengthen your self-esteem and sense of worth to healthier levels. However, before we consider the area of self-esteem and sense of worth, there is another area of focus that needs careful attention.

A lot of folks either forget or don't even realize that self-love also involves the spiritual aspect of being. There are three aspects of being that make up every human on this planet: 1. Physical and material, 2. Emotional and psychological, and 3. Spiritual. We need to strike an even balance between all three aspects. If we don't get that perfect balance, well we will just continue to feel like we're stuck ... like a truck stuck in the mud spinning its tires and getting nowhere. So how do you cater to your spiritual aspect of self?

It's simple enough: you pursue and nurture all of your general activities, hobbies, and interests. What are those things that you feel so strongly and passionately about? What makes your heart sing with joy when you think about doing them? The possibilities are virtually endless, but I will list just a few in order to get your minds and hearts going – to illustrate to you what I am meaning. So for example: painting, singing, dancing, photography, playing some type of sport or musical instrument, acting lessons, hiking and being involved with nature somehow, getting involved in animal advocacy and/

or care, horseback riding, joining a mutual interest group (such as Alcoholics or Narcotics Anonymous, Single Parents, local church gatherings and/or events, joining spiritual/metaphysical online groups or dating websites), pursuing and growing your own natural psychic healing abilities, yoga classes, book review panels, and so on. I could virtually go on and on and on. As mentioned the list is truly limitless in terms of examples, and not everything needs money either by the way. But the key here is to focus on activities and hobbies that *you* feel drawn to. Another key point to remember too is that you cannot limit or restrict yourself. Realize that your spirit in itself is part of divine source – therefore likewise limitless and non-restrictive. So why try to restrict something that by nature is limitless and without restriction to begin with? Try not to restrict your own divine nature, and nurture all those things that you feel drawn to. You don't have to be good at anything, you just have to love doing it!

The reason for nurturing yourself and pursuing those interests is triple-fold: as mentioned it gives balance to the spiritual aspect of being. But it *also* helps to build up those levels of self-esteem and sense of worth: the more you immerse yourself in and pursue your interests and desires, the happier you become and the more certain you will be of your path (now do you see why I said before we considered that area we needed to focus on the spiritual aspect of being?).

The third thing that this accomplishes, almost right from the moment we begin pursuing our interests, is it automatically opens up our heart centres (or heart chakras as many may refer to them as). Realize that it is from and within our heart centres where we ultimately send and *receive* love in our lives. Therefore it then stands to reason that the more our heart centres open, then ultimately the more love that we will in fact attract and receive in our lives! And love comes in many forms: job offers, new friendships, potential business partnerships, residential moves, pay raises, divine guidance and messages from spirit, *and love relationships*. Many different doors of opportunity begin to open up for us: so the more determined we are in pursuing those activities and hobbies and the longer we continue to pursue them, then essentially more and more doors will open.

By following my desire to pursue social work training, I actually attracted a few different forms of love in my life. Just a few examples: I attracted the money I needed to get through my schooling and support my children and I, I met my friend Mary, I connected with my mare Apache, and through those three events I ultimately met Martial. One door after another opened for me; which created quite the domino effect!

Change Your Search Methods & Criteria

There are a few things to note in this particular step. The first is you need to realize that every relationship experience (as well as all other kinds of human interaction) ultimately changes us. It doesn't matter what happened throughout the relationship, nor does it matter how it had ended. The main point is that the experiences and energy exchanged between two people changes them. That's why it is so important to take the time that you need in your healing and grieving processes that were discussed earlier; you need that time – and even the months following – to get reacquainted with yourself. Your likes and dislikes may have changed. Your beliefs and personality may have changed. Even your long-term goals may have changed. So it would then make sense that your needs and 'requirements' in a new love partner would change. Therefore you must base your affirmations and actual physical search on those new 'requirements.' A new relationship wouldn't work out too well at all if you didn't know the new you or if you continued to connect with partners who were carbon copy images of past partners. Past partners are in the past for a reason: they didn't work out – and there are reasons behind that. Maybe they drank too much, were too controlling, too wrapped up in their work, or perhaps too submissive? Whatever the reason, you most certainly don't want to repeat the past. So change up on your 'search criteria' in a new partner. Make an outline that somewhat reflects your own new character, personality, goals and interests. But in order to do that, you must first take that time to get to know yourself inside and out!

*As a note, an excellent example of a case where a person gets involved in a new relationship without first knowing their new self is that of the classic 'rebound relationship.'

The second concept goes somewhat together with the one above; change *how* and *where* you conduct your partner searches. If you don't want a partner who drinks alcohol, then you most certainly do not want to frequent any bars or nightclubs! That's just basic logic, yet some folks tend to not realize that. They say the definition of insanity is that of doing the same thing over and over again and expecting different results. So again, it is very important if you wish to actively search for a partner you need to base the search itself on your actual desires.

There is actually a third point that I do need to make here, and it may come as a bit of a surprise to you: the absolute most successful way to attract that very special someone is for you to actually not even concentrate on searching for them too much! It has been proven to me over the years with many of my clients – as well as with myself actually – that nine times out of ten your intended partner will come to you when you least expect it ... and when you're not 100% focused on them. The reason for this is simple enough: remember the concept of self-love. You cannot love another until you love yourself first. So, as you focus on yourself only and whole-heartedly pursue those hobbies, interests and general activities that we talked about earlier, you bring yourself closer to finding your intended partner. So the concept of not dwelling on a particular subject comes up yet once again.

I do realize that the addition of this third point may now add an element of confusion here. But if you think about it, it actually falls in line with outlining your search criteria to the new you and your interests, hobbies, etc. The key is to not dwell. To use an example, while I was yearning for a true love to share my life with, I was way too busy to fully concentrate on it. I wasn't actively looking (in honesty I didn't even know where the heck to look anyways). I was going to school, raising my children, working on the psychic website, and immersed in my activities with my horse Apache. I was solely focusing on myself – the idea of finding a life partner was clearly much further down on my list of priorities. It was there ... it just wasn't prominent. And then, out of the blue, Martial and I came together.

You see, the trouble with actively searching for a partner *all the time* and not focusing on oneself at all actually brings in the concept of a person trying too hard – especially when they are met with one unsuccessful partner after another (which often happens when that person doesn't allow the time they need to heal and get to know their new selves). When a person tries to force or tries too hard to accomplish something, that will actually create a block for them. In turn, this creates quite the vicious cycle of depression, frustration, *dwelling*, and negative thinking – which all then causes them to try harder and harder still. It's a horribly self-destructive cycle that I really don't wish to see anyone fall into. So that's why I brought up my third point: it's best to focus on yourself while you do in fact keep making affirmations and prayers for you to find that life partner. Be aware of your 'search requirements' in a partner and keep your heart open to receiving that love, but do not dwell on it! Your prayers will be answered in time: the more you pursue your interests and hobbies, then the more tools you will in fact give Divine to use to help you.

The Law of Attraction & Reprogramming the Mind

"I'll never find that special someone." "I'm always going to be alone." "No one will want to date me let alone marry me when I have two kids." "I'm not very attractive." If that's your way of thinking, then you're right. You won't find that love, you will always be alone, you won't find someone who is truly attracted to you, and you won't find a partner who accepts your children. I hate to be so darn harsh, but I needed to stress the importance of how your thoughts and feelings do in fact create your reality. So I'm going to say right here and now: if you're thinking like that or have any sort of negative thoughts about yourself and/or the future ... STOP IT!!!! You're just blocking yourself from all that you actually desire!

Besides ... who put those particular beliefs and thoughts into your head to begin with? Who made you think so negatively about yourself? Was it your past partner? Or one of your parents? Where are they truly coming from? If you think about it, you didn't always feel that way. So in all seriousness, those are not your thoughts ... they are someone else's. Somewhere along the way, someone came along and 'rewired' or 'reprogrammed' your mind like they would a second-hand computer. That is actually an excellent way to look at your mind: let's say you bought a used computer from a friend, but that friend didn't take the time to reformat the hard drive ... or at the very least didn't delete all of their personal files. To make matters worse, you also notice that the computer has a Trojan virus. Now you're stuck with those files, programs and virus for the moment. What are you going to do with them? Are they of any use to you? Should you use the computer with a virus eating up the programming? No! The virus is going to totally annihilate the operating system, and like I say that computer's programming and settings are someone else's. So in order to personalize that computer you're going to have to either reformat the hard drive or delete all the files yourself and install an anti-virus. Your mind and your way of thinking is exactly the same. You need to 'delete' all those thoughts and beliefs that truly do not serve you ... and are not even of your own creation. Essentially those thoughts and beliefs are riddled with the 'virus' as well. So do you still want to hold on to them?

Are you not a free spirit? Is your spirit not infinite and divine? Do you not have your own desires and emotions? Of course! So why continue to hold on to someone else's 'programming' that's full of a nasty 'virus' when you do have your own to operate with? Change your programming to your own – which is a much cleaner, more accurate, and positive version.

You ARE beautiful. You ARE worthy. You ARE strong and intelligent. And you DO have a very special someone out there waiting for you.

With that having been said, you need to remember that the Law of Attraction is at work in our lives whether we realize it or not ... and whether we want it to be or not. For those who don't fully understand what the Law of Attraction is, it is the basic spiritual law which states that whatever we put out there into the Universe we attract more of. So all of our worries, fears, sense of lacking, and negative self-talk just attracts more to be worried about and fearful of. Just as one example: if you're always worried about money and feeling like you never have enough money, you will essentially attract more money troubles. So in keeping with the context of this book, if you say to yourself that you'll never find that special someone, well ... you won't because you're making the Universe believe that this is what you're wanting. Whatever your focus is, the Universe will respond and give you what you're focusing on ... even when those thoughts and beliefs that we talked about earlier aren't your own! That's why it is so important for you to take the time to reprogram your mind to your own sets of beliefs and thoughts!

So instead of always focusing on the negative, focus on the positive! Make the Law of Attraction work in your favor instead of working against you. Be thankful for what you already do have in your life so that you will attract even more to be thankful for. Be firm in the belief that you *will* find that special someone and that you *are* worthy of love. Actually, take that a step further and adopt the attitude that you *already have* that someone in your life. When you do that, you essentially "trick" the Universe into believing that perhaps it messed up or has been caught sleeping on the job – so it'll step up the pace to try and match that energy frequency that you're emanating (ha ha – sorry but that's the best way for me to describe the concept to you).

I don't advocate for anything that I personally do not believe in or haven't had a first-hand experience with. So when you see me talk about the Law of Attraction ... hey ... I am telling you straight up that it is very real and it does work. What I will say here though is that of course it can be difficult to maintain a positive attitude all the damn time. Of course you're going to have those negative thoughts and feelings once in a while – which indeed will counteract all of the positive that you have in fact put out there. So what you do, once you catch yourself that is, you immediately state, *"I retract all previous negative affirmations, thoughts and statements."* And then you add your positive statement or affirmation right afterwards.

Let Go & Forgive Yourself and Others

This particular step can only be accomplished once you have completed your healing and re-learning process, and have come to the realization that no matter what has happened in your life, it all happened for a reason (or reasons) that we may not even be aware of. In actuality, all relationship experiences are divinely meant to occur. But understand that just because something may be divinely meant it doesn't mean that any given relationship was supposed to last forever. Each and every connection ever made between us and another individual teaches us valuable lessons, allows us to grow, and ultimately molds us into the people we are today. Therefore every person we have ever connected with has played a major role in our evolution as spirits.

In realizing this profound concept, you need to let go of any anger, resentment, or any other negative emotion associated with particularly bad relationship experiences. Holding on to those emotions just continues to hurt you – not the other person. It also creates a rather significant spiritual or energetic block when it comes to you successfully reaching future relationship goals. Let go and forgive others who you perceive may have wronged or hurt you – for they were only operating as sculpting tools for Divine. Realize though that forgiveness is not forgetting. Nor is it condoning or excusing what the other person has said or done. Likewise, forgiving doesn't obligate you to reconcile with the person who harmed you, or release them from legal accountability. Instead, forgiveness brings you peace of mind and liberates you from those harshly negative emotions such as anger and resentment. It empowers you to recognize the pain you suffered without letting that pain define you ... enabling you to heal and move on with your life.

Letting go also includes the very important concept of not holding on to the past – to not keep looking back or dwelling on past events. Take the lessons learned, leave the rest, and then move forwards. It's a lot like driving a vehicle: you're driving down a long stretch of highway towards a certain destination. But instead of paying attention to what's going on up ahead of you, you're always looking in your rear-view mirror. If you're constantly looking in that darn mirror, you're never going to see what's in front of you! This can lead to true disaster as I'm sure you of course realize. Well, the same can be said for progressing down your life path: if you're always looking behind you instead of looking ahead, you're setting yourself up for the very strong likelihood of missing out on many amazing opportunities (or pitfalls for that matter). I would have to further state here too that it will also cause major issues in any future relationship that you may have.

It took me a long time to forgive Mark (and many other people in my life). I also had a hard time letting go of my past. And in being human, yes of course I do still sometimes fall into that resentment rut. However, I quickly pick myself up and out of it because I know full well that everything that I have ever gone through in my life has brought me to the here and now ... and I wouldn't trade my current life for anything in this world. I'd do it all again if I truly had to.

Life Path Divine Sequential Order: Everything Happens for a Reason

In May of 2012 I received quite the profound gift of insight during one of my nightly meditation sessions. The very next day I had to write an article about it in my blog – to try and pass along the information Divine had given me. The term "life path divine sequential order" was actually given to me during that meditation. I am including the majority of that article here as it greatly supplements the advice given in this book – especially when we consider the concept of letting go and allowing forgiveness for oneself and others. Once we realize that everything does have purpose and reason – even the most negative of events, it makes it slightly easier for us to accept and let go:

Life Path Divine Sequential Order:
It's Not All Coincidence How I Met
My Life Partner & Soulmate

Everything happens for a reason. That I am sure of. Even the most horrible of experiences in life happen for a reason – but of course in those moments we're definitely not willing to accept this concept.

But at the end of the day, once we get through it all (and we always do get through it), if we reflect over our pasts we can realize the amazing sequential and divine order that has occurred ... and throughout our ENTIRE lives. Each and every situation and event – both positive and negative ones – whether created by ourselves or by someone else in our lives – it all has divine purpose (which leads us to bigger and brighter things later on). Did you know that even your very own thoughts, decisions, actions and inaction they too all have divine reasoning – causing this eventual sequential order? That means that there are NEVER any mistakes in life. But in knowing this, it kind of challenges one's beliefs when it comes to free will doesn't it? I do still wonder just how much free will we do have – especially in having the profound insight that what we THINK is free will actually isn't. Here now I am going to try and illustrate this concept to you – please bear with me but we DO get to a point eventually...

This is my story – well – a very brief outline really considering a lot of what I myself have had to go through it would most definitely fill an entire novel.

I wish to share my story with you because like I mentioned a moment ago; when I reflect over it all I can see how my path has led me to the here and now. Every action I took, every decision I made, and even things that I experienced due to the actions of others ... ALL OF IT led me to where I am today: divine reasoning leading to life path sequential order. Take out just one event or action ... I often wonder where I would be. Obviously not here!

While my entire life path has most certainly contributed to where I am today – a lot of "crap" was experienced in childhood as well. But I will spare you the gruesomeness that was my life back then and just for the sake of this article, begin when I was a young teenager and my relationship with my ex-husband.

I was fifteen when I first met and started dating my now ex-husband. Such a young age! Of course at that age I refused to listen to any of my elders and would go out of my way to be with this man (of whom was/is 22 years my senior!!!). I was too wrapped up with the "coolness" that he was a hard core biker who hung around with other bikers – it was a party type of lifestyle almost every weekend. And I was drawn in ... even though I never did drink or do drugs I was still entranced by all of it. Understandably my elders were very concerned – they even tried to stop me by reporting to police. But I wouldn't listen and the police wouldn't help either. So I continued on ....and in having knowledge within psychology today I do realize I was "looking for daddy" (as I didn't know my biological father until I was 24 years old).

At the age of 17 I gave birth to my first-born baby (this is another story in itself but due to my age and lifestyle I was coerced into putting her up for adoption. We have reunited however – about 2 years ago now). After her birth I moved out of province with this man (who is her father of course) – moved away from all my family and away from all that I knew.

We remained together for approximately 14 years ... with another 3 children having been born in that time (a boy when I turned 20 and then twin girls almost 5 years later). But those 14 years were not the happiest in my life. Sure, there were good times. However, quite frequently I was subjected to my then husband's dominance; he was very controlling, domineering and abusive – while I don't ever like to make excuses I have to admit that it was always the drugs and alcohol that would cause this psychotic type of behavior to rise up within him. Sober he was an "okay" guy. But drunk he was quite obnoxious, abusive and controlling – especially to any woman or love partner that he is currently involved in (I feel sorry for the women he may have been with since our separation if they've had to deal with even an ounce of what I had to).

Leading up to the end of our marriage I grew increasingly resentful, angry and hateful towards him and my life. It was to the point where I hated him to even touch me. Believe me when I say that it is quite the awful feeling to have towards another person ... especially when that person is your own husband. Now, to top it off I want you to take a few steps back for a moment and remember something: I was 15 when we first started out together. So just to add to it all, because I became involved with someone so early in my life – I literally missed out on the learning, growing, and experiencing that a normal teenager and girl in her early 20's would normally experience. As a result I was yearning for more for myself; feeling that I have missed out on so much. So that added to my own negative attitude.

The nightmare finally ended in November of 2003 – where he went way too far and the police were called in. That was the beginning of the end and the start of a new beginning for me...

We sold our home and I moved to where I am now the following June. I moved a total of 8 hours away and straight north!!! Why??? Well, I will get to that ... there were reasons that I wasn't even aware of at the time ...

Before I came to the strong realization about the concept of what I call "Life Path Sequential Order," I would always question, "Why me?!" "Why did I go through all of that?" Why didn't I listen to my elders all those years ago and just behave like a good girl? Why was I so defiant?" "Why did I move out of province with him? Why did I put up with that horrible abuse all those years? Why did I move so far away now? Why did I come to a community where I can't even get work because I am not completely bilingual? Why did I buy such a money pit of a house? Why why why why?!?!?!"

Well today, I can tell you why ... at least for most of it.

It wasn't because I was being a little brat or "trash." It all happened for a reason.

All of the abuse that I suffered – I now use that experience to draw upon when I am counseling other abused women and clients. I can relate to them in ways that even some counselors cannot. I understand their thinking processes and reasonings. I can also understand that trials and hurdles that they must overcome in being single mothers after they leave their relationships/marriages. I needed to experience the abuse so that I could have that understanding – so that I could better guide those in need. I wouldn't have ANY of that valuable insight had I listened to my elders all those years ago and hadn't moved with him, etc.

When it comes to moving a total of 8 hours away as a single mom with 3 young children in tow, originally my plans at that time, were I wanted to get as far away from him as physically possible ... and ... the price was right for the house where to this day although I still experience some financial difficulties, I do not have to pay any mortgage or rent. I own this house outright. However, unfortunately I was so wrapped up with the idea of remaining a homeowner and in the end saving myself a monthly expense.

As the years progressed, I was given even more reasons why I moved so far north. Had I not moved here ... I would not have met and subsequently married my intended life partner and soulmate!

In 2006 I purchased a mare and due to an argument that I had with the property owner's boyfriend, I then *required a new place to board her – and immediately! A friend of mine suggested "this guy" … well "this guy" came a mere hour after calling him with his horse trailer and we moved Apache to his farm. That was in September and we were becoming friends over the next few months.*

But, in January 2007 my mare Apache spooked in the barn as he reached up to turn the light on … and she kicked him right square in the face; breaking his jaw in several places and dislodging his left eye out of its socket. I caught word and raced to the hospital as soon as I could … he was a mess. I remember holding his hand, crying and apologizing to no end. As I left I gently kissed him good bye and I remained at the farm to tend to the rest of the horses for him.

Upon returning home after his surgeries he wasn't able to do any lifting at all, so I would help with feeding the horses and household chores. Our relationship began to take on a new form … and we started dating not too long after (not long at all because I recall wanting to be with him for Valentine's day!)!

Then, to add insult to injury … quite literally … we were forced to move from the farm and sell all the horses as the farm was sold out from underneath him (he was only renting at the time and he couldn't find another farm). So that was yet another harsh experience to go through … and by August of that same year (2007) I found myself opening my doors of my home to him and he moved in. And we've been together ever since!!

We were married, on horseback in a cowboy style wedding, August 23, 2008.

EVERYTHING that I had gone through with my ex-husband, my moving here, Martial's accident with Apache ... ALL of it happened for a reason. If none of that happened – we wouldn't be where we are today. Quite literally. Think for a moment – had I not stayed with my ex-husband all those years to suffer the abuse, I wouldn't have been inclined to move so far away from him upon separation. Had I not married my ex to begin with, would I have had the money to purchase this house here? Not likely. Then again, I would have had no reason to purchase it to begin with.

Had I not remained with the ex, I wouldn't have been blessed with my four wonderful children. In fact, consider I may not have had any children at all if things were different. If I had no children but still met Martial those many years later, I wouldn't have had any because not even a year after we married I was diagnosed with cancer and as a result I had to have a hysterectomy to remove it. I am extremely thankful that I was given the opportunity to have children ... and long before I had to have that hysterectomy!

And I don't think I need to mention that if I hadn't moved here, I wouldn't have purchased Apache and thus never met Martial. His accident, while absolutely horrifying, it was the catalyst that brought us together as a couple – and even more so when he was forced to move from the farm. If he hadn't moved in with me, I wonder if he would have proposed on Christmas Day like he had (which believe it or not was only a few months after he moved in!).

As mentioned earlier, I still question why this particular house ... why I bought it even though it's so old and direly needing very extensive repairs. But in seeing and knowing the divine sequential order that has taken place throughout my entire life, I am hopeful that this too is also for a reason or reasons that will most likely become apparent later on.

You can go back to the very beginning of your life when it comes to divine sequential order. For example I didn't know my biological father until I was 24. If I had known him as a child, perhaps I would not have even gone with my ex-husband (consider his age and lifestyle. My father would NOT have approved and he would have stopped it!).

It's so very hard to keep the perspective that everything happens for a reason ... especially when we're right in the midst of the chaos and events. But one thing to note is that we will never experience something that doesn't have reasoning behind it – nor will God ever put us in a situation that we would not be able to handle.

Throughout those trying years I often cursed those situations. However, now I am extremely thankful for my entire life path. If it weren't for those experiences and moments in time ... who would I be? Where would I be? God only knows where I'd be.

I now don't really wish that I could "turn back the clock" to do things differently. Quite frankly, I am extremely grateful for where I am, what I have, and who I am with. Who knows, without having traveled that rocky road I might have wound up in even worse situations ... or never would have met my intended life partner.

I believe the old adage is true: "The rockiest of roads often lead to the most rewarding destinations in the end."

Try to keep that in mind whenever you face a difficult situation or life event. While it may not be immediately apparent, there is divine intent behind it... no matter whether it was your decision or the decision of another ... and it WILL at SOME POINT lead you to something bigger and better later on down the road.

And by the way ... had it not been for me even separating from my ex-husband those years ago, I would not have met anyone else in the online metaphysical field ... I wouldn't even have worked at a very well-known psychic website, nor on my own website here! It was our separation that made me take action for myself and look for work. Only 2 weeks after my separating from my ex-husband I landed my second and most significant online psychic job!

And here's a last tidbit for you: the second year that I was living on my own here I decided to put myself through schooling in order to obtain a degree in social work and psychology. Well ... little did I know there was divine reasoning and intent behind THAT decision too! Remember the "friend" that I mentioned earlier who suggested I contact "this guy" to board my mare Apache? Well, I met that "friend" in school!!! Had I not gone to school, I wouldn't have met her at all – and once again I would not have met my husband Martial! She was the one that ultimately introduced me to him.

Everything happens for a reason ... and almost always for reasons that you don't even know about or realize until later on!

Paradise Found: New Love Relationships & How to Make Them Succeed

7 couldn't possibly write this book without including at least a few pointers for when you do in fact connect with that very special someone. Of course each individual relationship experience is unique, but there are a few basic "universal rules" to remember that can help you progress within the relationship itself more successfully and comfortably.

Every Love Will Be Different

This is one lesson that I personally learned relatively quickly: no matter how hard you try you will not *ever* experience the same kind of love twice. I have had a number of clients come to me to 'complain' that while they adore their new love partner, it just doesn't 'feel the same' as what they had experienced with a past partner – and that they yearn to have that same love again. Well ... no. It won't feel the same ... and it never will. It won't matter who you are with, you will experience different dynamics and levels of love. I know that this is a rather hard pill to swallow, but it's just the way it is. If you're wanting to experience that same feeling of love, then unfortunately you're going to have to return to that ex-partner because that's the only way you'll be able to fulfill that particular desire (and if that ex-partner was toxic and/or abusive in any way, then I definitely do not encourage you to do so!).

Every person is unique – therefore every relationship will be unique. Each and every relationship experience will have its own set of dynamics and its own energetic vibration. Once you come to a place of understanding and acceptance of this basic truth, you will then set yourself free from that restrictive viewpoint and will be able to truly embrace and enjoy the new relationship connection that you have in front of you.

There is No Comparison

This concept can actually go together with the one we just discussed. Just like you will never experience the same kind of love twice, you will likewise not ever connect with a partner who has the same type of personality and/or interests or talents. In other words – as mentioned a few moments ago – every person is unique. As a result, it just isn't fair for you to make comparisons between your past partner and your new partner. It's not fair to you, and it most certainly is not fair to them. So don't make those comparisons, and don't try to change your new partner! Accept them for who they are. You need to keep in mind that Divine brought that new partner into your world just as they were – and for a reason!

As horrid as it sounds, believe it or not I actually had a few people approach me when I first started dating Martial who asked me why I was with him. Sure he was a great guy and very popular in town, but he had no money, he lived in a true ramshackle of a wee home, he was a workaholic, and he had an addiction to marijuana. Do you know what I said to those nosey people? *It's none of your damn business!* Everything that they said was true yes. But I didn't care! I loved him for who he was. And while I did start to compare him to my ex – I immediately caught myself. There was really no point because they're like night and day. They both have good points and they both have bad points. So yet another small reminder: no one is perfect. We all have flaws and we all have strengths. It is therefore pointless to try and make comparisons.

Another point to make here is to also remember that just because your ex-partner hurt you a certain way, that does not mean that your new partner will do the same thing. They are not your ex-partner. They are not the past. As it was mentioned earlier: leave the past behind and focus on the present.

I know what has been said here is something of a 'no-brainer' for many folks and you're likely saying to yourself, "Well of course they're not the same." However, all of us do make those comparisons on some level – and many don't have that conscious awareness of what they're doing. If you've ever experienced even just one other relationship in the past ... well you've made those comparisons. Everyone's 'guilty' of it to some degree. It's normal to make some comparison. The difference here though is that if you're not careful, you just might get a little too caught up in it ... and eventually it *will* be picked up on by your new partner – which in turn *will* cause some friction between you.

Let Go of the Controlling Reins

This is one of the most difficult concepts to master – as human beings we feel like we need to have control over everything that's going on around us. Especially when it comes to growing new relationships and we're eager to reach ultimate success! Not only do we want to know what will happen, where it is going, how will things progress, and when, we also have the urge to actually control or steer the relationship in the direction we want it to go ... and we even try to control the pace at which the relationship itself will grow!

It needs to be understood though that the very moment we ask those questions and start to try and control direction and pace, we automatically form expectations within ourselves: expectations of the relationship and expectations of our new partners. And in having expectations, depending on the circumstances we could essentially be setting ourselves up for disappointment and hurt; which is something none of us need when we've already been hurt in the past!

In beginning any new relationship, the absolute best way to enter into it is for you to remain in a rather neutral position emotionally-speaking. Do not force the relationship to progress any faster than what it's naturally supposed to progress. Doing so could potentially cause you and/or your new partner to "freak out" and actually create distance between you! And just as importantly, do not project into the future. So in other words don't try to figure out where the relationship is going. Live in the moment and take each day as it comes to you. You can't enjoy the new connection if you're always wondering where it's going to lead. Adopt the attitude of, "Who cares? As long as I'm enjoying myself that's all that matters. If something becomes of this then it's just a bonus."

To stay in the present moment does not mean you should never think about the past or responsibly plan for the future. The idea is simply not to allow yourself to get lost in regrets about the past or worries about the future. If you are firmly grounded in the present moment, the past can be an object of inquiry. You can attain many insights by looking into the past. But you must still remain firmly grounded in the here and now. To live in the moment means just to not get swept away by the future and past, so that we forget to experience the beauty of the present.

A few small points need to be added here though with this particular piece of advice: 1. Don't be over-analyzing your partner and/or the relationship, 2.

Don't go looking for trouble when you have had no real cause to (because trouble will often find you if you do – remember the Law of Attraction! This can be hard when we've suffered great heartache, but we can't allow our fears to dictate our futures), and 3. Allow your new partner to meet you in the middle when it comes to effort (so in other words for example it isn't advisable that you call or text them every single day – give them space and make them initiate communication once in a while! Also allow them to make date plans, etc. Don't always be the one to make plans or demands. Compromise and take turns.). Those three concepts are also forms of control that we do need to let go of.

I did have a bit of a hard go with this one – I did find myself wondering where my relationship with Martial was going to take me. However, I believe one of the keys to our success was indeed that of allowing the space and time that *both of us* needed. No matter how much I wanted to, I didn't 'chase after him' all of the time – I allowed him to initiate communication at least 50% of the time. I was also quite well aware of my insecurities that had formed from my experience with my ex. I was hoping so much that the relationship would last. Yet, one of the main concerns I had was that I didn't want to repeat the past. Even though I loved the new connection and how it made me feel, I was fearful that perhaps I had fallen for another abusive man. But on the other side of the coin here, I also knew that Martial himself had some rather terrible past relationship experiences. So both of us needed that time and patience in order to gain trust with each other; I wasn't overbearing – I tried to remain neutral with him, but I reciprocated his advances when he made them to ensure that no mixed signals were sent his way. And that's an important point to remember as well: keep in mind that your new partner may have had some rough experiences of their own that they are still recuperating from – therefore all the more reason to just take things as they come: one day and one step at a time.

As hard as what it is to not control the trajectory of the relationship, I just cannot stress to you how important it actually is to let go of that desire. You'll be taken in whatever direction Divine has in store for the two of you. Just enjoy the ride!

Self-Awareness

This one is pretty much self-explanatory. Always be aware of your own processes, emotions, and ways of thinking. It is especially important to take notice of any residual effects that may have been left behind by an upsetting or abusive relationship – and work on them before they come back around and bite you in the behind! For example, even two years after I married Martial, unfortunately I still had an issue of control and possessiveness over my personal belongings. Don't check my mail ... I'll check it myself thank you. Leave my truck alone ... go get your own. Don't ask me who I'm talking to on the phone when I'm actively on the phone ... if I want you to know then I'll tell you all about it after

I hang up. In that same thought, you don't need to ask me where I'm going ... I'll always tell you and if you're not here before I leave, then I'll leave a note just in case. Don't tell me what to wear unless I ask for your input. Don't make plans for renovations in this house without first consulting with me. To this day I also have problems when it comes to negative energy: any anger, yelling, or upset of any sort and I'm running to the bathroom sick. That one I believe I will always suffer from (as it wasn't just due to my past marriage – the 'bad nerves' also comes from an abusive childhood as well as being a very strong empath and energetically sensitive), but at least with the control and possessiveness I've seen tremendous improvement. But you see? I had those particular 'problems' that were created. However, I was fully aware of them and where they had come from ... and I knew that if I let them overrun me then ultimately they would ruin my relationship with Martial. Furthermore, Martial was also fully aware. So together, as a team, we worked to eliminate them the best we could. On that note, this now brings us to the next and last point of our discussion ...

Open & Honest Communication

Not too much can be said with this particular pointer. Everyone knows that the most important key to developing any successful relationship is that of establishing and maintaining a strong level of open and honest communication. However, I know that this is probably one of the most difficult to master – especially when we've been raised and/ or conditioned in our childhoods and/or past relationships to hide our emotions and thoughts. Due to that restrictive past, a fear has been deeply engrained within us which dictates that the moment we speak our minds we will ultimately 'suffer the consequences.' But we're not in those restrictive positions anymore, and we need to remember that! Not every partner is like our past partners; in the vast majority of cases our new partners *want to know* how we're feeling and why, what we're thinking, and even what our dreams and goals are. In fact, many partners – like Martial – actually feel deeply hurt and even sometimes disrespected when we don't 'come clean' about all that's on our minds. Us withholding our innermost feelings, thoughts, and desires ultimately sends the misunderstood message that perhaps we don't want them to get too close to us (which of course is the furthest thing from the truth. But they don't know that!). So with that said, not openly and honestly communicating will also lead to a lot of confusion and misinterpretation – which could then in turn very likely lead to an abrupt ending of the relationship.

Thankfully Martial was (and still is) very patient with me on this one. Even though we've been together for a number of years and I have in fact improved quite a bit, I still have trouble in telling him how I'm feeling and what I'm thinking. In fact, once in a while I will *still* start out my statements with either, "Please don't get mad, but I ..." or the tentative, "Uhm, honey. Can I say something?" I'm sometimes nervous, but at least I do tell him what's on my mind.

So don't ever be afraid to share your goals, feelings, and thoughts. It will bring the two of you closer together as a couple; it will deepen the love for one another and the two of you will gain a tremendous amount of trust for each other. Oh! And just as importantly: always communicate with gentle love and honesty. In fact, you may be pleasantly surprised; your partner will likely take part and share their own thoughts, feelings and goals with you! An otherwise uneventful day could essentially be turned into one of the most memorable heart-to-heart moments in your relationship. Yet on the other side of the coin, I also have to say that the communication shared will also show the two of you whether you're on the same page or not. If the two of you don't have understanding for each other or share the same long-term goals (such as marriage for example), then it's best to get that out into the open right away so that neither one of you go on to feel like you were lied to or strung along.

* As a note: Please remember that some new partners will also have a block or trouble with their own effort in open and honest communication. However, the more that *you* make an effort to come forward and open up, then the more your new partner might appreciate your efforts and will actually try to follow suit. Sometimes we will find ourselves in a bit of a teacher role. One of the best ways to teach is to of course be patient, but just as importantly, to demonstrate or model the principles

and/or ideas ourselves. In cases such as this, in the beginning it is a good idea to watch/study your partner's body language, underlying tones in their speech, and their behaviors. Also take the time to feel the energy that they're putting out; you'll feel a strong uneasy, upset, or nervous energy. You will generally know when something is on their mind or they have something to say. Usually you just posing the question, "Is something bothering you?" will encourage them to spill the beans; if not immediately then certainly given a small amount of time once they gather the courage. Asking the question lets them know that you wish to hear what they have to say, without judgment or repercussions, and even possibly help them in some way.

The Tug-of-War

Up and down. Back and forth. On and off. Hot and cold. They're here but then all of a sudden they're not here. What is going on? Well I shall tell you: these are "classic" signs of someone who has a very powerful fear within their subconscious that's holding them back from ultimately moving forward in the relationship. These fears can include that of fear of commitment, fear of failure, fear of change, fear of letting go of bachelorhood, fear of repeating the past, and so on. I've included this particular concept in this book simply because there is a good chance that either, 1. Our new partner may have this problem, or 2. We might be the ones giving this behavior to our partners without even realizing it. So with that said, it is always good to have that awareness (remember the concept of self-awareness!). I have seen this particular issue countless times over the years with my clientele; it is quite the frustrating situation for the person who wishes to move forward, and I've felt quite often that if the person only knew what they were doing and why, well they could then consciously work to eliminate the fearful behavior.

The cause of this seesawing behavior is actually quite the complicated psychological process (which was caused by the person not having allowed themselves enough time to heal and go through the motions of letting go, forgiveness, and all the other concepts mentioned earlier). The person is fighting a huge battle of tug-of-war within themselves. On one end of that rope you'll find the positive: their love and their desire to commit whole-heartedly. On the other end of the rope are all the negatives: their fears and uncertainties, haunting memories of the past, the hurt they experienced before, and so on. And in the middle? That is where you will find them. And they are being yanked back and forth between the two in quite the painful and tormenting manner. When they are yanked over in favor of the positive, those are the times that the relationship is going well and/or they return from their absence (the "off" periods). When they are tugged towards the negative side, that is when they create distance and out of the blue decide to "disappear" for a period of time.

The Tug of War, if actively worked on by both partners and given some amount of time and patience, it can definitely be won! No matter what this is not the easiest of roads to travel. But essentially this situation could be greatly avoided if the person would just give themselves the time to heal and go through the motions of letting go and forgiving.

Pick Your Battles

This is a loving reminder for you to remember that you do not need to show up to every battle that you might be invited to! Just because someone may be having an "off" day and may start to nit-pick at you as a result, that does NOT mean that you should feed into their already negative mood and energy by snapping back at them. This would just cause more drama and stress that neither one of you need in those moments. It is best to just walk away and allow some peaceful time to rest and relax.

This is also a reminder that when it comes to emotionally or energetically "off days," sometimes it is best to not address particularly troubling or upsetting/stressful news or thoughts. Nor is it the time to continue any arguments. Leave things alone if you find yourself or your love partner somewhat off kilter emotionally. When energies and moods have calmed, the dust has settled, and emotions have balanced once more, that will be a better time to do so. "Calculated timing" is the best practice to remember.

Picking your battles however also means to realize which "arguments" are truly worth the time and effort. Leave matters that were already resolved in the past alone, and try to avoid the "nit-picking."

Other Points of Interest & Insight to Remember

Like a Sponge Sopping Up the 'Good Stuff'

*A*s it was mentioned earlier, a very important realization that you must eventually come to is that *all* relationship experiences are divinely meant to occur. It doesn't matter if it they were great relationships or very toxic ones – they were all meant to happen. All of them are 'divine connections.' They shape us into the people we are today. However, what I didn't mention earlier is that eventually, all of those relationships – including your relationship with your parent and siblings, will also help you to 'form' your ultimate life partner. I was given this very interesting tidbit of insight late one night during one of my routine meditation sessions: you will find that your divinely intended life partner will share similarities with past partners and parents, and may even have exact polar opposite traits as well. It's like you walked along your life path with a sponge in your hand, but only gathered up all the best traits or personality offsets along the way! Let me try to illustrate this interesting concept to you:

I look at Martial and I realize that he is a true 'mix' of a number of different relationships that I've had throughout my life. My biological father was pure French, and he also had what I called a rather irrational anger that would be triggered by literally nothing – and indeed quite out of the blue. Obviously Mark had the anger, too. Well, Martial has both of those traits, but at least when it comes to the anger he has that awareness about himself – and if he doesn't catch himself in time he always apologizes. My stepfather and half-brother were quite the avid hunters and fishers. Again Martial has those traits. Then there was a gentleman that I didn't write about in this book; he hired me to work on his book series as a freelance editor (another career attempt that obviously didn't work out). He formed a romantic interest in me as time went on, but I quickly squashed that 'dream' of his by outright refusing to reciprocate his advances ... and eventually ended the entire connection with him. However, this man was extremely spiritual. He believed in the metaphysical: psychic abilities, energy work, spirits, reiki, and so on. He was also quite 'touchy' emotionally-speaking where he felt emotion very deeply ... and he definitely had no qualms of showing his emotions and/or talking about them (and if felt deeply enough he would indeed fly off into a bit of a temper tantrum). I remember feeling so darn uncomfortable ... I didn't even knowing what to think, say or do whenever he flew off into one of those 'emotional outpourings.'

They were extremely intense, but I believe what caused this extreme level of emotion is the fact that years prior he had suffered from a major head injury. It was so severe that he had to take pills to regulate the chemicals in his brain for the rest of his life. When I look into Martial, he has all of these traits too. Except the difference is that Martial has a comfortable balance; he isn't intense, he doesn't make me feel uncomfortable, he always talks calmly and rationally about his feelings, and he doesn't have to take any sort of pills for his numerous head injuries (which were suffered as a result of being a horse trainer most of his life. You play with horses, you're bound to get hurt).

When I look deeply into my beautiful husband, I can see a part of almost every past male connection I've ever experienced – I could keep going with the list if I really wanted to, but I think you get the point. While I know it's very difficult to not curse all those past relationship encounters (God knows I've done it myself many times), you need to remember this vital concept: Divine has just been preparing you for and leading you towards your ultimate destination! So with that being said, this could very well be a major 'clue' for you to watch out for: if you can see numerous comparisons and/or similarities in your partner (not just one or two ... there has to be a larger number than that), then you can likely assume that you have indeed found your intended life partner. But just as a note, as it was mentioned earlier in the book if you find that your current partner is a *spitting image* of a negative past partner with absolutely no offsets and he or she makes you just as uncomfortable as the past partner, well that should of course tell you they may not be 'the one.' Remember – no mirror images or carbon copies. Past partners are in the past for a reason!

Life Path Divine Sequential Order – Take Two

I wish to focus for a few moments once more on the concept of Life Path Divine Sequential Order, because that does greatly compliment the idea that every relationship is divinely intended. As it was mentioned: *everything* happens for a reason.

With that concept in mind, I have come to realize and accept that I wasn't being a self-destructive, indignantly blind brat who constantly made the wrong choices or mistakes. Not even my analytical questioning and psychological reasonings of my behaviors matter. Sure, they obviously do have some weight and truth behind them: for example it's a well-known school of thought that women who were severely abused in childhood tend to gravitate towards or attract abusive love partners. I experienced severe physical and sexual abuse as a young child. So yes I'm sure that may have something to do with what I went through in later years. But the thing is, there are different aspects of being that we need to consider. As we all have physical bodies, we also have spiritual bodies. Therefore there are always "physical" reasons as well as "spiritual" reasons for everything. To illustrate this for you further, for example we form conscious reasons why we are going to move into a particular house or city. Perhaps it's the price of the home, the general cost of living is lower, or it is closer to our place of employment. Those are "physical reasons" why we would say or do something. However, later on we may learn that we moved into that house or city because it led us into finding our intended life partners, reunited us with beloved members of our soul groups, or the energy of the location "agreed with" our spiritual energies and thus raised our entire energy vibrations – which in turn allowed us to further ascend and even make psychic abilities a hundred times stronger. Those are "spiritual reasons" that are found behind all actions/inaction, decisions/indecision, behaviors/ thoughts, and so on.

I want you all to remember that there is no such thing as making mistakes. Nothing is a mistake ... you never make a 'wrong choice,' and nothing was ever a 'waste of time' – not even a past relationship. *It all happened for a reason!* Hmm ... I believe I have the makings of a second book right there. I will have to seriously consider this and discuss it with my guides.

Developing Psychic Abilities Amidst the Chaos

During the critiquing of this book, one very observant and spiritual reviewer had asked me, "How did you develop your psychic abilities and connection with Divine when you were in the middle of such chaotic conditions? You should include that in the book for I'm sure many others would have the same question."

Well, I will tell you something: when you are in an abusive and/or unfulfilling relationship, and likewise didn't experience true nurturance and love from parents in childhood, you yearn to have that unconditional love. When I first started my meditation practices and connected with my spirit guides, I found that unconditional love with them. They didn't judge me. They guided me without question. They didn't chastise me for anything I perceived as having done wrong. Yes they were stern at times, but they always gave me that unconditional love. They grounded me, comforted me, and encouraged me. Within my spiritual space, spending time with my guides, I felt safe and full of joy. I always came out of meditation anxiety-free, determined, and happy. So as a result, well as mentioned at one point earlier I think I made quite the pest of myself. I was always meditating and connecting with my guides – quite often just to feel that strong and purest of pure love. I craved it – almost like an addiction to drugs or alcohol – so I connected with them as often as I possibly could. As a result of that constant connecting, automatically it strengthened my abilities. And that happens for everyone ... chaos or no chaos. The more you meditate, connect with your guides, actually follow the guidance/advice given by your guides, and *utilize* your abilities, then the more the abilities themselves will strengthen.

However, it does seem that when we're actively involved in the chaos, sometimes we actually grow much more quickly than others who are in "more balanced" situations. But that's only because in those moments we are placing our entire hearts and trust into Divine. We are open to receiving the guidance, and well to be honest with you we're also too tired to even be bothered to question or second-guess Divine's instructions! So with that said, admittedly I grew exponentially in the last year of my past marriage. After I left Mark, they levelled off somewhat, but then again approximately three years later I experienced another growth spurt. Oh yes by the way – get used to those growth spurts! We all get them ... and they happen for our entire lives. Once the gateway is open and you are almost constantly allowing traffic through back and forth (asking for psychic insight and receiving psychic insight), well then there is no stopping the growth. I have been reading professionally now for over twenty years and I am *still* learning new concepts and growing.

I have had my psychic abilities since early childhood (clairvoyance, clairaudience and clairsentience), so I also had a bit of a 'head start' so to speak when I decided to connect with my guides and Divine source. However, one thing that I did notice as I started to seriously focus on growing my abilities throughout the earlier years of my past marriage was that I seemed to pick up on mainly negative events that were to occur – or warnings if you will. And they always gave me this horribly nasty sense of 'impending doom' that I would feel from the tip of my tailbone all the way up to the back of my neck. I would feel it so strongly that oftentimes it would send me into quite the bout of anxiety and panic ... to the point where I would then develop the shakes and feel physically ill to my stomach. There are two reasons for this: 1. Due to our ancient human traits or dna inherited from early man, we have a natural 'flight or fight' programming. As a result of this natural human trait, we are wired to detect even the most subtle energies that would be of a threat to us and our well-being. If there is any amount of danger coming towards us we of course want to steer clear and take cover, or conversely fight our way through it. We want to be prepared long before it arrives. Therefore, quite often beginning psychics will pick up on those warnings before anything else as they come through more strongly and immediately. 2. Constantly living in a negative environment (in my case I experienced childhood abuse and then spousal abuse), we become conditioned to always expect some sort of negative event to occur. So on a subconscious level that's of course the first thing we're going to look for.

If you find yourself experiencing the same as what I had, in order to broaden your perspective from just picking up on the negative you have to change your way of thinking – stop focusing on the possible negative outcomes because that's exactly what you're going to get! Focus more on the positive outcomes ... and your desires to move forward. You also need to ask your guides and Divine to show you or allow you to feel more positive messages. Besides, only feeling and/or seeing negative messages certainly wouldn't help you to progress along your life path would it? It actually doesn't give you any direction to follow at all. I remember saying in my mind, "Why do I always just get the doom and gloom? I've had enough of that! I need true direction. I need answers and guidance that will propel me forward ... not silly warnings that will hold me back!" I believe almost instantly my abilities were broadened ... just by making that extremely firm statement and consciously looking out for the more positive messages and signs.

* As an added note, one other thing that helped me tremendously in my early psychic and spiritual development was the frequent use of gemstones and essential oils. While there are many gemstones that have psychic ability enhancing qualities, I swore by my lapis lazuli stone necklace. If you feel the desire to implement the use of gemstones, some others to consider are: bloodstone, azurite, carnelian, amethyst, calcite, fluorite, emerald, labradorite, malachite, moonstone, quartz, sapphire, turquoise, and snowflake obsidian. As a word of advice, only select stones that you feel strongly attracted or drawn to. If you don't feel drawn to them and just grab any old stone just for the sake of, then there will be the strong likelihood that they won't work as well for you ... if at all.

When it comes to essential oils, the main ones that I used were sandalwood and sage. There are numerous kinds of oils that you can use; some of which come in an excellent "perfume" that can be applied to the physical body – which I used as well. I encourage you to search metaphysical shops in your area or online for oils that you feel drawn to.

Don't Give Your Personal Power Over to Psychics

Did I just surprise you with that subtitle? Those who know me wouldn't be too surprised at all; as an ethically-practicing psychic I refuse to tell people what to do, I refuse to make decisions for people, and I refuse to interfere with a person's learning of important life lessons. Learning about who you are, what you are capable of, what your life purposes are, and ultimately who you should be with in a love relationship are all divinely intended life lessons that must be learned by the individuals themselves. I can and will guide you best I can, and I will of course try to help give direction on where to look or what to do for example. But I won't just outwardly tell you what you *must* do. Understand my meaning here?

The allure of getting psychic readings is strong when we're in rather murky waters – which is fine ... I try to help guide folks the best I possibly can as it is good to receive some amount of insight. Readings can definitely be excellent tools to help folks make more informed decisions for themselves. However, for decades people have been asking psychics like myself questions such as, "Who is my soulmate? What is his or her name? What does he or she look like? What is his or her career? What is his or her astrological sun sign? When will we meet and how?" I will tell you: I cringe when I receive those types of questions, and cringe even more when I hear about psychic readers giving answers to those questions. Why? Because it takes away that person's power. It interferes with their free will and learning of those valuable life lessons. Furthermore, the very moment a psychic does answer those questions, they greatly restrict that person's perspective. If a psychic tells a person that their intended partner will have blue eyes, black hair, works as a dentist, has the letter 's' at the beginning of either their first or last name, and that they will meet in a nightclub – well guess what: some folks will greatly narrow their search down to only concentrate on those specific criteria that the psychic outlined. What if the psychic was wrong? What if it was a rather 'shady' or 'bogus' psychic just spinning a few yarns? What if the psychic you consulted with was operating from a place of ego and actually told you traits that *they* look for in a partner? What if you go to two or three different psychics and they all give you different answers? Then what? Well, my guess is that your search will never end ... or it will be greatly hindered at the very least

Don't place such restrictions onto yourself, and don't throw away your own good sound judgment and personal power. Finding your own empowerment and awareness of self is one of the most powerful feelings in the world. I just cannot describe accurately enough the profound levels of happiness, power, inner peace, and satisfaction that one feels.

Psychics are great resources for obtaining insight into situations, for helping to establish future paths and/or for pointing a person in the right direction, but they shouldn't be used to make actual and absolute choices or decisions. Make your own *informed decisions* based on the psychic insights received. And if a psychic tries to tell you that your intended partner has specific traits, don't hold that information as being golden. Base your partner search *only on your own requirements and personal insight!*

Meditation to Meet Your Spirit Guides

While this particular meditation/visualization was originally developed to meet animal totem guides, I have received numerous reports from clients that I've referred this to that it likewise works very successfully with all forms of guides and angels – including meeting crossed over loved ones. So if you don't wish to meet an animal guide but prefer an angel or other life form, that's perfectly fine. Just replace your meeting intention of the animal guide with whomever you wish!

As a note, the best way to do any form of visualization is to not force anything to happen. Try to think of your visualization as a movie that you're watching: you can pause it and can even rewind it if you have to. But you do not have any control over the storyline or the outcome. Just allow whatever to flow to you naturally and on its own. So don't try too hard ... and don't force – you'll just block yourself and make it even worse. I also don't really recommend doing any meditation or visualization when you're tired or have way too much on your mind. I don't know how many times I've done that where I've ended up falling asleep before any of my guides can even say a single word, or I don't even make it there because my monkey mind had other plans and took me all over the place (I remember one time, I finally made it to one of my guides; she just stood there with her hand on her hips, shaking her head at me and laughing. Ha ha!).

Sit on the floor or lay comfortably in your bed and totally relax. Close your eyes, breathe deeply and slowly, and allow all of your muscles to completely relax. Now visualize your Crown Chakra (which is located on top of your head or just above it – and is a large orb filled with the most divine white energy/ light). Once you have your Crown Chakra visualized quite clearly, next visualize a chord of this very same light/energy flowing from your Crown Chakra down through the top of your head, traveling down along your spine, all the way down through to the Earth. Visualize this energy moving down even further, deep to the core of the Earth and connecting with it. Feel the warm energy of the Earth flowing through your body and feel its power increasingly strengthen you. Allow this energy and power to surge through your entire body: your arms, legs, fingers, toes, and so on. Allow the energy and power to build within you, until you create a slight "energy/power cocoon" that envelops your entire body (this should be seen as a slight aura (or energy field if you will) made of the similar energy that is now flowing through you – emanating approximately an inch or two in thickness from all around your body). Once you have visualized this, you may now allow the darkness behind your eyelids to envelop you. Visualize a white light shining up ahead of you. Begin to visualize yourself walking toward this light. As you get closer, notice that you are walking towards a doorway to another realm. Interesting... What does that door look like to you? What is it made of? When you open this door, look out and see a beautiful, lush forest and step out onto the ground. Take in your surroundings: look at the trees, shrubs, grass, weeds, flowers, etc. Are there any streams or rivers around? Walk around to enjoy and explore everything that is surrounding you. As you look ahead of you, you see a pathway through the trees. Visualize yourself stepping onto the path and beginning to walk slowly. Walk a while, and then pause. Then listen carefully and wait. Soon you may see your animal guide approach you. Take as much time as necessary ... until your guide finds you. When you see this animal, speak with him or her. Ask any question you might have in mind – perhaps even ask him or her what their name is. Or, maybe you just want to say hello at this point. It is your decision. When your animal guide motions to you that your meeting is finished, politely thank him or her and say goodbye (my first meeting with one of my guides I gave him the biggest hug!). But please, also make sure that you promise your guide that you will return once again (in order for your relationship to flourish with your guide you do need to make it a common practice).

Walk slowly back to the doorway you passed through and visualize yourself walking back through it. Step into the darkness once again, and see another light up ahead. Walk to the light, and visualize it slowly enveloping you and surrounding your entire body. Once the light surrounds you, you may then open your eyes. At this point your journey is complete. I would then perhaps take the opportunity to write down all that you saw, all that was perhaps said between you and your guide. Anything that you feel was quite significant ... write it down. Because if it doesn't make much sense to you now, it just might later on down the road!

*** One thing to note though – if you have more than one spirit guide, only one may come through to meet you at a time. Within my own experience (as at one time I had three different animal guides), that was indeed the case. During meditation and a "meeting" with one of my guides, I noticed a rustling in some bushes in the not too far distance. I also got the feeling of being watched quite closely – as well as feeling some sort of "expecting" or "eager" type of energy waiting for me behind those bushes. But all the while, nothing emerged from there. When I ask, even as I write this article, as to WHY another guide refuses to emerge while you are already sitting with one, I just get the very stern message that it is "private" and that it is "polite and respectful to do so." So, when you meet your first guide for the first time, politely ask him/her if there is any other spirit wishing to meet with you. If the answer is yes, then you will indeed be urged to "set up another meeting" for your other animal guide(s). I met my animal totem.

A Final Word About My Journey

As of writing this book, it is right now the end of July, 2015 – just three and a half weeks before our seventh wedding anniversary. Our three sons have graduated high school; my 21 year-old son has moved out to British Columbia and works as a roofer (hopefully that doesn't last much longer and he'll return to go back to college!), and Martial's eldest boy has a job working as a heavy duty mechanic in a gold mine not too far from home here. We have just one more high school graduation to go: my twin girls' – who will be graduating next year. My one daughter is aspiring to become a registered nurse, while the other is undecided between either an accountant or air traffic controller. And Martial's younger son, he too is undecided: either an electrician or a game warden – he's taking this year off to make his decision.

Folks are probably wondering what happened to Mark. Well, he passed away very suddenly from quite the aggressive liver cancer. We still kept in contact all these years. Even after everything said and done, we maintained a good friendship right up until 'the end.' Even Martial forgave him after some time and grew close to him. However, for the entire time that I was a single parent and well after I married Martial, Mark still didn't send a single dime in child support – except at Christmas two years in a row he sent a gift to each of the kids and a grocery gift card to me (which strangely was the Christmas of my and Martial's engagement and then our first Christmas as a married couple). He would never call, and most certainly never came to visit after that Easter in 2006. As a result of Mark's clear unwillingness to accept responsibility for his three children, Martial and I decided to go through a legal step-parent adoption process. Martial was providing for and loved my children as they were his own anyways ... so why not make it official? But that process, for both my children and I, was more of a test too for Mark – to see if he would finally take action. Much to everyone's surprise – including the presiding judge's – Mark didn't do *anything*! By law the courts not only had to notify Mark of the adoption and call him to court (serve him papers – which they did), Mark also had to give an answer – whether he consented to the adoption or not. All Mark had to do was to just pick up the phone to call either our lawyer or the courthouse itself and say 'no, I do not consent.' Just the word 'no' would, by law, make the judge cease the proceedings and not put the adoption through. But he didn't even do that! The judge went as far as postponing the proceedings for an additional month to try and give Mark time to respond. Even then Mark did nothing. So after a month's delay, the judge called all of us into his chambers and granted the step-parent adoption. As a result of this adoption, Mark lost all parental rights – including the right to see and/or speak to the children (unless Martial and I consented to it). He could not have any contact with any of the children until they reached the age of 19. After the adoption went through, it's funny but Mark would try to demand to see the children ... right up until his time of passing. He just didn't accept the fact that my children didn't even have a strong interest or desire in seeing him. Remember what I said a while ago? How he had been digging his own grave? Well ... there we have it. My son is almost 22 now, and has blatantly stated to me that he had no interest. As far as my girls go, they share their brother's attitude. But can you really blame them? It's very sad. I felt bad for him and always updated him on what the kids were doing, but unfortunately he did it to himself.

As a result of what transpired with those people where I boarded Apache, Martial thought it best that I sell both her and the baby Serene – we just didn't have anywhere else to take them (and to be honest Martial was having a very difficult time re-bonding with Apache since his accident – he disliked her greatly and the only thing he did like about her was how, as he says, she brought me to him – I caught him whispering that to her one day when he was trimming her hooves). It broke my heart, but I couldn't argue with his reasoning. I had no choice, and I certainly didn't like the energy that was being exchanged between Martial and Apache. It was best that she go to a new home. My last memory of Apache was of me going out to meet her and Serene out in the pasture; I called out to her and immediately she started cantering towards me ... with little Serene, then three months old, trotting close behind her. But she was in heat again – and the other fifteen horses knew it. So next thing they *all* start galloping towards us. Oh crap! I started to run as fast as I could as I didn't want to get kicked or trampled – and this was the magical part: Apache ran right along with me – her nose within inches of my shoulder but not once did she step on me with her feet or try to run me down. We ran together – for the last time as two spirits combined into one.

I was so devastated the day I sold her: I could hear Apache crying and whinnying all the way down the long driveway and up the road as they drove away with her in the trailer. Even now I sit here and cry as I recall those final moments. I felt like I had betrayed her. I loved her so much – I still do love her ... and always will. And I will likewise always be forever thankful for her having led me to my divinely intended soul mate and life partner: Martial.

Martial and I are still living in my century-old home (yes my house turned a hundred years old this year! And wow, I can't believe it's now been eleven years since I first came to Iroquois Falls). Our goal, pretty much ever since we lost the ranch in 2007, has been to get back on the farm where we belong – and I wish to start up a horse rescue and rehab operation once we do. We miss our horses terribly, and at this point would do almost anything to have them once more. It's been hard hanging in there, but in reflecting over my past and how Divine always managed to help me fulfill my dreams one way or another, I know that eventually we *will* have that farm!

Our beloved Sheba, Martial's female yellow lab, passed away at the golden age of fourteen in the winter of 2012, and our old boy Max, Martial's male yellow lab, just passed away not long ago, ironically the same age as Sheba was at her passing. We also have a few new additions to our family: Bella and Lingo – two labradoodles, Alex my Alexandrine parrot, and Zeus my African Grey Parrot.

Married life with Martial – well like pretty much every married couple we have our ups and downs. That's normal and to be expected. However, I am so proud to say that for the first time in my life the happy and positive days greatly outweigh the unhappy and dark ones. Not a day goes by in this house where we're not laughing about or doing something stupid, and Martial is still up to his old antics and telling of big stories (although at this point *none* of us believe them and half the time you'll hear one of the kids walk by and jokingly call their dad a loser): no honey you are *not* old enough to have been in the Vietnam War, you did *not* get attacked by a crocodile in Meadow Creek, and you did *not* teach every famous wrestler all their best moves.

We both work very hard: Martial continues with his farrier work and horse training (which I assist him with when I can), and he also has a very busy and successful landscaping/home improvement business. And me ... well you know me. I've long since left that online psychic website that I started working at in 2004 and have been focusing more on just my own official website ... which has kept me on my toes – trying my absolute best to guide and provide insight wherever needed. My specialty does seem to be that of relationship readings, and I bring in a lot of the skills that I learned throughout my studies in the social work program that I had taken. I regularly appear on numerous radio shows, and am even in the beginning phases of creating a unique relationship oracle card deck for all to use!

What's so awesome too is that I also finally have a husband that supports my spiritual beliefs and psychic work (and shares my interest in the paranormal, haunting investigations, and such) – however at times I've had to tell Martial to simmer down and be careful who he told. Not everyone accepts or believes in the metaphysical. So perhaps he can be a little too eager at times (but I love him all the more for that). Martial is also quite the adept animal communicator, so there have been a few occasions when he has worked alongside me in my working with animals and their spirits.

Martial has also stuck by me through some of the most life-changing events: 1. Remember how I vowed that I would find my first-born daughter? I kept my word to her – I found her one week after her nineteenth birthday thanks to the government opening adoption files with identifying information. Within receipt of those documents, it literally took me five minutes to find my little girl. She has since moved to be closer to me, and we visit as much as we can. 2. Not even a year after Martial and I were married, I was diagnosed with micro-invasive cervical cancer. As a result of this – and as a preventative measure – I had to have a total hysterectomy performed (and that was after we had decided that I would go and get a tubal ligation reversal so that we could have one last child together). Today thankfully I am cancer-free. 3. Remember me mentioning my horrible teeth and the incident where I got stuck at the dentist's office because Mark didn't put me on his benefits? And how he had knocked out two of my teeth in our Night of Reckoning? Well over the years as a poor single mother, my teeth degraded to the point where not only did I refuse to smile, but I was suffering from abscess after abscess. I became very sick last October with what was the absolute worst abscess of my life – it actually scared the crap out of me. So I found a dentist who was compassionate enough and who would work with me, and well to make a long story short I went through the nasty process of having major dental surgery – there was no saving any teeth so they were all removed and immediate dentures were placed. As of writing this I am six weeks out of surgery, and still trying to get used to the change.

Martial pretty much supports me in anything I wish to do – for so long as it is within reason of course! And I do the same for him. I just cannot imagine my life without Martial now – and it isn't because of that old feeling of before where I thought I needed a man for security. I'm my own person and have the power to handle anything Divine decides to throw my way. No ... it is because I love him with all my heart and spirit. This is what true love is all about: instead of fearing how you are to pay the bills when he's gone or fearing that you can't make it alone, you're dreading the thought of not being able to hold his hand, give him a hug and a kiss, listen to him snore next to you in bed, put up with him stealing all the covers on a cold winter's night, or to hear just one more frustrated French curse word or silly story about his so-called life in Vietnam. And I would, without hesitation, put my life on the line in order to protect that man. That's love ... and it is out there for all of us to find. All of us have that one special 'butterfly-giving cowboy man or girl' out there waiting for us to find them. And while I know better than what I'm about to say, sometimes I just can't help it: I wish I had learned all of the valuable life lessons that I've just passed along to you today so much sooner ... and without all the heartache and pain.

That has been just a small part of my journey ... and it isn't over yet!

As a final added note: many people have asked me how I got through such times in my life and state how strong of a woman I had been. For many years I actually didn't have an answer for them (and admittedly I had a hard time accepting their well-meaning compliments). I just didn't know how to answer other than the fact that I simply followed the divine guidance that I was given despite the fears that I held. However, the *real* answer finally hit me a few months ago. So now if you ask me how I got through, this is going to be my answer:

Happiness is a choice. You can either choose happiness and pure joy, or you can simply roll over under a rock and essentially die. All these years I thought that I just did what I had to do for myself and my children. Sure. I did that. That's true enough. However, take a few moments and look deeper into that: *I did what I had to do because on a subconscious level (and likely spirit level too) I had already made my choice. The choice to be happy.* All the steps I took and the decisions I made, I made them because I had already made that choice for myself. I didn't just accept what was. I didn't get stuck in a depressive pity party for myself. Like I say I didn't know that then – I just believed that I did what I had to in order to live. But I know it now. It wasn't just to live. It was to thrive.

About the Author

Lisa Caza

Celebrity Psychic Clairvoyant, Tarot Reader, Expert Love Psychic & Animal Communicator

*L*isa has been practicing her clairvoyance, clairsentience, and clairaudience abilities since early childhood. Even though her family was full of skeptics ... she was determined to not let them sway her. It was not until one day, when she was 11 years old, that she "foretold" to her now-late grandmother that there would be a tornado in their area that day, that her family then realized her wonderful talent. As it turned out ... unfortunately for many unwary folk ... there were in fact fourteen tornados that touched down that evening – three of which were within the same vicinity of each other. Bringing much destruction and devastation to the areas, that day will not soon be forgotten ... especially by young Lisa.

Lisa is known world-wide for her honest and sometimes rather blunt clairvoyant readings. Yet at the same time her messages are always full of love, wisdom, and compassion for all. Lisa has been a professional psychic reader for over 20 years, and regularly appears on numerous popular radio shows – including the nationally-syndicated Outer Limits of Inner Truth. Lisa is also an experienced relationship psychic counselor and social worker, and has even further experience in Canadian Family Law and child protection issues.

For Lisa, her work in the metaphysical field is all about being able to assist those in true need. While it is the law that all practicing psychics must post the disclaimer "For Entertainment Purposes Only" on their websites, Lisa takes her work very seriously and stresses that she does not like to be used as an entertainment unit. For her, it is all about alleviating one's sorrow or pain, passing on positive messages and profound insight, stating truths and honest messages rather than sugar-coated "stories", revealing a person's options and pathways, helping a person gain understanding strength and knowledge, and giving a light to shine so that they can better see the path that lays before them. Seeing the people that she's helped grow, become empowered and ultimately succeed actually gives her the greatest of rewards.

Lisa lives and practices from Northern Ontario, Canada; however folks from all over the world connect with her in order to seek guidance in love, relationships, family, careers, finances, and even insight into past lives and yearly predictions. She is also an extremely gifted animal communicator and "occasional medium."

Learn more about Lisa Caza and her work by going to her official website, following her on Twitter, subscribing to her blog, and joining her Facebook fan page.

Website: www.lisacaza.com

Twitter: www.twitter.com/Lisa_Caza

Facebook: www.facebook.com/SoulPsychics